The Upgrade Keto Diet

Cookbook for Beginners

1800	Quick & Easy Low-Carb Homemade Cooking Recipes - Help Lose Extra Body Fat with 30-Day Meal Plan

Daniel K. Shannon

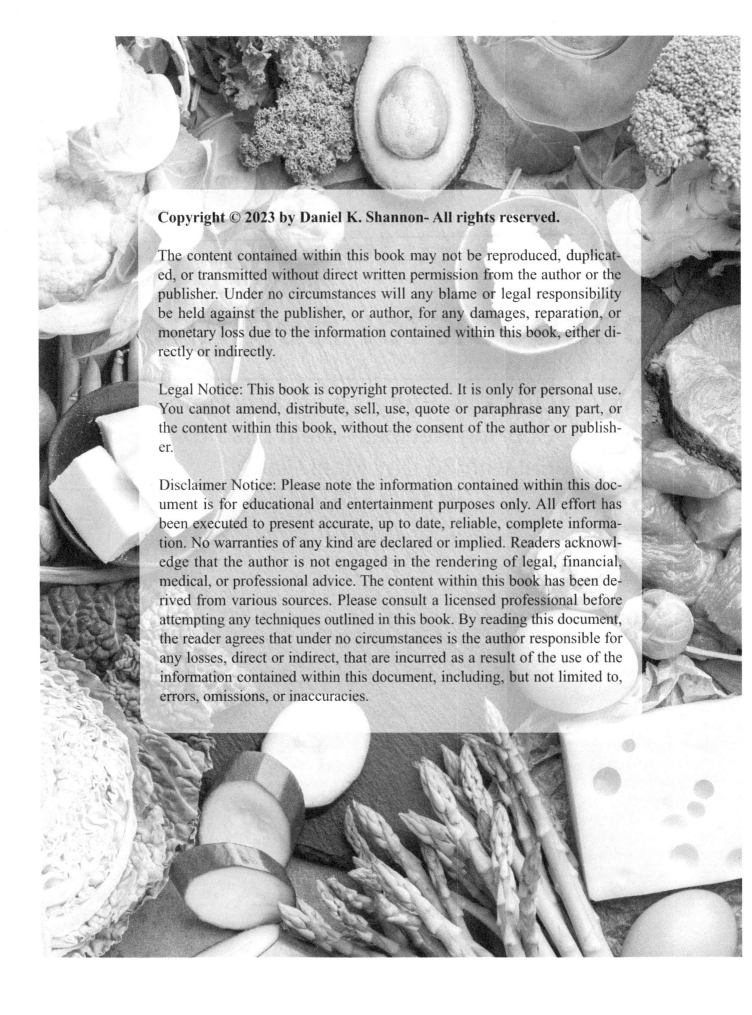

CONTENTS

Soups, Stew & Salads Recipes 62

Desserts And Drinks Recipes 73

INTRODUCTION

Daniel K. Shannon, an esteemed advocate of the ketogenic diet, the Keto Diet Cookbook, written by him, explores the transformative power of the ketogenic diet. This book is your guide to a healthier, more energetic lifestyle, all through the wisdom of a low-carb, high-fat dietary approach. Welcome to Daniel K. Shannon's Keto Diet Cookbook.

He has curated a selection of recipes that are as delicious as they are nutritious. By prioritizing fats and minimizing carbohydrates, these dishes align with the principles of the ketogenic diet, a strategy that promotes weight loss, boosts mental clarity, and offers a host of other health benefits.

The cookbook reflects Shannon's commitment to healthy living and his passion for creating meals that nourish the body and please the palate. Whether you're a seasoned keto devotee or just starting your journey, this book equips you with everything you need to thrive on this diet. You'll find satisfying recipes, helpful tips for maintaining a keto lifestyle, and insights into the science behind this revolutionary diet.

The recipes within these pages cater to all tastes and dietary needs, proving that a shift towards a ketogenic lifestyle doesn't mean a compromise on flavor or variety.

Join Daniel K. Shannon on this gastronomic adventure and discover the many benefits that the ketogenic diet has to offer. Here's to your health, happiness, and culinary delight!"

What is the Keto Diet?

The keto diet is a revolutionary approach to eating that flips traditional diet advice on its head. Rather than emphasizing low fat and high carbohydrates, the keto diet promotes a low-carb, high-fat intake, turning our understanding of nutrition inside out. As a distinctive dietary strategy, the keto diet prioritizes fats as a primary source of energy, constituting about 70-75% of the daily caloric intake. Proteins make up about 20%, while carbohydrates are limited to a sparse 5-10%. This approach triggers a metabolic state known as 'ketosis', where the body efficiently burns fat for energy instead of carbohydrates. The result? Potential weight loss, increased energy levels, and improvements in various health markers. It's a fascinating shift from conventional wisdom, redefining our relationship with food and exploring the health benefits that a new macronutrient balance can offer. It's a diet that's sparked much interest due to its potential benefits including weight loss, improved heart health, better blood sugar control, and in some cases, enhanced mental performance.

What health benefits can I expect from Keto Diet cookbook?

• **Weight Loss Support**

By offering a plethora of keto-friendly recipes, this cookbook facilitates the process of weight loss. The ketogenic diet shifts the body's metabolism from carbohydrates to fats, promoting efficient burning of body fat.

• **Heart Health**

The Keto Diet Cookbook champions recipes rich in healthy fats, such as avocados, olive oil, and fatty fish, which can aid in lowering 'bad' LDL cholesterol and elevating 'good' HDL cholesterol, thereby supporting cardiovascular health.

• **Blood Sugar Regulation**

The recipes in the cookbook contribute to better blood sugar control, providing a practical resource for those managing or preventing type 2 diabetes. By restricting carbohydrate intake, the diet can help reduce blood sugar levels.

• **Enhanced Mental Clarity and Energy**

When your body is in ketosis, it produces ketones—a powerful energy source for the brain. Using this cookbook to maintain a state of ketosis could lead to improved mental focus and energy levels.

• **Reduced Inflammation**

The keto diet has anti-inflammatory properties due to its high antioxidant content. This may offer protection against various chronic diseases, including certain cancers and neurodegenerative disorders like Alzheimer's.

II

What kind of food is included in the Keto Diet?

Meat and Poultry

Unprocessed meats are low in carbs and high in fats, making them suitable for a keto diet. This includes beef, pork, lamb, chicken, turkey, and game meat.

Fish and Seafood

Fatty fish like salmon, sardines, mackerel, and trout are keto-friendly. Other seafood such as shrimp, crab, lobster, and squid can also be included in the diet.

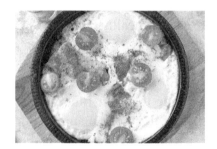

Eggs

Eggs are high in protein and fats, and very low in carbs, making them a great option for a ketogenic diet.

Dairy

High-fat dairy products such as cheese, butter, heavy cream, and full-fat yogurt are often included in the keto diet.

Healthy Fats

Avocados, olives, and oils such as olive oil, coconut oil, and avocado oil are high in healthy monounsaturated and polyunsaturated fats.

III

Nuts and Seeds

These are high in fat and low in carbs. Almonds, walnuts, flax seeds, pumpkin seeds, chia seeds, etc., are often included in a keto diet.

Low-Carb Vegetables

Non-starchy vegetables like spinach, kale, broccoli, cauliflower, zucchini, bell peppers, cucumbers, etc., are low in carbs and high in fiber.

Berries

While most fruits are high in carbs, berries are relatively low in carbs and high in fiber, making them suitable in small amounts.

Spices and Herbs

Most spices and herbs are low in carbs and can be included in a keto diet for flavor.

30-Day Meal Plan

Day	Breakfast	Lunch	Dinner
1	Spiced Gruyere Crisps 6	Spiced Pork Roast With Collard Greens 16	Grilled Cauliflower 50
2	Grilled Cheese Bacon Jalapeno 6	Beef Meatballs 16	Cauliflower Mac And Cheese 50
3	Crispy Chorizo With Cheesy Topping 6	Paprika Pork Chops 17	Creamy Almond And Turnip Soup 51
4	Parsnip And Carrot Fries With Aioli 7	Creamy Pork Chops 17	Spaghetti Squash With Eggplant & Parmesan 51
5	Middle Eastern Style Tuna Salad 8	Spicy Spinach Pinwheel Steaks 17	Zucchini Boats 52
6	Keto "cornbread" 8	Habanero And Beef Balls 18	Egg And Tomato Salad 52
7	Cranberry Sauce Meatballs 8	Swiss-style Italian Sausage 18	Keto Cauliflower Hash Browns 53
8	Keto-approved Trail Mix 9	Pork Osso Bucco 19	Roasted Brussels Sprouts With Sunflower Seeds 53
9	Party Bacon And Pistachio Balls 9	Cocoa-crusted Pork Tenderloin 19	Roasted Asparagus With Spicy Eggplant Dip 54
10	Apricot And Soy Nut Trail Mix 9	Warm Rump Steak Salad 20	Grated Cauliflower With Seasoned Mayo 54
11	Choco And Coconut Bars 10	Garlic Pork Chops With Mint Pesto 20	Creamy Artichoke And Spinach 55
12	Bacon Jalapeno Poppers 11	Meatballs With Ranch-buffalo Sauce 21	Zoodles With Avocado & Olives 55
13	Pecorino-mushroom Balls 11	Beef Tripe In Vegetable Sauté 22	Creamy Kale And Mushrooms 55
14	Boiled Stuffed Eggs 12	Garlicky Pork With Bell Peppers 22	Colorful Vegan Soup 56
15	Tart Raspberry Crumble Bar 12	Bistro Beef Tenderloin 23	Greek-style Zucchini Pasta 57

Day	Breakfast	Lunch	Dinner
16	Coconut And Chocolate Bars 13	Hot Pork With Dill Pickles 23	Creamy Cucumber Avocado Soup 58
17	Zucchini And Cheese Gratin 14	Beef Brisket In Mustard Sauce 23	Zucchini Noodles 58
18	Sour Cream And Carrot Sticks 15	Balsamic Grilled Pork Chops 24	Cream Of Zucchini And Avocado 58
19	Sausage Links With Tomatoes & Pesto 21	Charred Tenderloin With Lemon Chimichurri 25	Vegetable Tempura 59
20	Parsley Beef Burgers 24	Easy Thai 5-spice Pork Stew 25	Roasted Leeks And Asparagus 60
21	Blackened Fish Tacos With Slaw 44	Adobo Beef Fajitas 26	Greek Styled Veggie-rice 61
22	Sausage Roll 57	Beef With Dilled Yogurt 26	Cauliflower Fritters 61
23	Keto Enchilada Bake 59	Beef Bourguignon 27	Brussels Sprouts Salad With Pecorino Romano 62
24	Spinach Fruit Salad With Seeds 66	Easy Chicken Vindaloo 28	Corn And Bacon Chowder 62
25	Sour Cream And Cucumbers 66	Pacific Chicken 28	Simplified French Onion Soup 63
26	Green Mackerel Salad 68	Easy Bbq Chicken And Cheese 29	Bacon And Spinach Salad 63
27	Chocolate Cakes 73	Spinach Artichoke Heart Chicken 29	Creamy Cauliflower Soup With Bacon Chips 64
28	Raspberry Creamy Smoothie 73	Paprika Chicken With Cream Sauce 30	Arugula Prawn Salad With Mayo Dressing 64
29	Choco-chia Pudding 74	Avocado Cheese Pepper Chicken 30	Traditional Greek Salad 65
30	Lemony-avocado Cilantro Shake 74	Buttered Duck Breast 30	Lobster Salad With Mayo Dressing 65

APPENDIX : Measurement Conversions

BASIC KITCHEN CONVERSIONS & EQUIVALENTS

DRY MEASUREMENTS CONVERSION CHART

3 TEASPOONS = 1 TABLESPOON = 1/16 CUP

6 TEASPOONS = 2 TABLESPOONS = 1/8 CUP

12 TEASPOONS = 4 TABLESPOONS = 1/4 CUP

24 TEASPOONS = 8 TABLESPOONS = 1/2 CUP

36 TEASPOONS = 12 TABLESPOONS = 3/4 CUP

48 TEASPOONS = 16 TABLESPOONS = 1 CUP

METRIC TO US COOKING CONVERSIONS

OVEN TEMPERATURES

120 °C = 250 °F

160 °C = 320 °F

180° C = 350 °F

205 °C = 400 °F

220 °C = 425 °F

LIQUID MEASUREMENTS CONVERSION CHART

8 FLUID OUNCES = 1 CUP = 1/2 PINT = 1/4 QUART

16 FLUID OUNCES = 2 CUPS = 1 PINT = 1/2 QUART

32 FLUID OUNCES = 4 CUPS = 2 PINTS = 1 QUART

 = 1/4 GALLON

128 FLUID OUNCES = 16 CUPS = 8 PINTS = 4 QUARTS = 1 GALLON

BAKING IN GRAMS

1 CUP FLOUR = 140 GRAMS

1 CUP SUGAR = 150 GRAMS

1 CUP POWDERED SUGAR = 160 GRAMS

1 CUP HEAVY CREAM = 235 GRAMS

VOLUME

1 MILLILITER = 1/5 TEASPOON

5 ML = 1 TEASPOON

15 ML = 1 TABLESPOON

240 ML = 1 CUP OR 8 FLUID OUNCES

1 LITER = 34 FL. OUNCES

WEIGHT

1 GRAM = .035 OUNCES

100 GRAMS = 3.5 OUNCES

500 GRAMS = 1.1 POUNDS

1 KILOGRAM = 35 OUNCES

US TO METRIC COOKING CONVERSIONS

1/5 TSP = 1 ML

1 TSP = 5 ML

1 TBSP = 15 ML

1 FL OUNCE = 30 ML

1 CUP = 237 ML

1 PINT (2 CUPS) = 473 ML

1 QUART (4 CUPS) = .95 LITER

1 GALLON (16 CUPS) = 3.8 LITERS

1 OZ = 28 GRAMS

1 POUND = 454 GRAMS

BUTTER

1 CUP BUTTER = 2 STICKS = 8 OUNCES = 230 GRAMS = 8 TABLESPOONS

WHAT DOES 1 CUP EQUAL

1 CUP = 8 FLUID OUNCES

1 CUP = 16 TABLESPOONS

1 CUP = 48 TEASPOONS

1 CUP = 1/2 PINT

1 CUP = 1/4 QUART

1 CUP = 1/16 GALLON

1 CUP = 240 ML

BAKING PAN CONVERSIONS

1 CUP ALL-PURPOSE FLOUR = 4.5 OZ

1 CUP ROLLED OATS = 3 OZ 1 LARGE EGG = 1.7 OZ

1 CUP BUTTER = 8 OZ 1 CUP MILK = 8 OZ

1 CUP HEAVY CREAM = 8.4 OZ

1 CUP GRANULATED SUGAR = 7.1 OZ

1 CUP PACKED BROWN SUGAR = 7.75 OZ

1 CUP VEGETABLE OIL = 7.7 OZ

1 CUP UNSIFTED POWDERED SUGAR = 4.4 OZ

BAKING PAN CONVERSIONS

9-INCH ROUND CAKE PAN = 12 CUPS

10-INCH TUBE PAN =16 CUPS

11-INCH BUNDT PAN = 12 CUPS

9-INCH SPRINGFORM PAN = 10 CUPS

9 X 5 INCH LOAF PAN = 8 CUPS

9-INCH SQUARE PAN = 8 CUPS

Appetizers, Snacks & Side Dishes Recipes

Spiced Gruyere Crisps

Servings: 4
Cooking Time: 10 Minutes
Ingredients:

- 2 cups gruyere cheese, shredded
- ½ tsp garlic powder
- ¼ tsp onion powder
- 1 rosemary sprig, minced
- ½ tsp chili powder

Directions:

1. Set oven to 400ºF. Coat two baking sheets with parchment paper.
2. Mix Gruyere cheese with the seasonings. Take 1 tablespoon of cheese mixture and form small mounds on the baking sheets. Bake for 6 minutes. Leave to cool. Serve.

Nutrition Info:

- Info Per Servings 2.9g Carbs, 14.5g Protein, 15g Fat, 205 Calories

Grilled Cheese Bacon Jalapeno

Servings: 2
Cooking Time: 40 Mins
Ingredients:

- 8 ounces cream cheese
- 2 tablespoons grated Parmesan cheese
- 1 1/2 cups shredded Cheddar cheese
- 16 whole jalapeno peppers with stems
- 8 slices bacon, cut in half crosswise
- Oil spray
- 1 1/2 teaspoons garlic powder

Directions:

1. Preheat a grill over medium heat and brush grill grates with oil.
2. Combine cream cheese, Parmesan cheese, cheddar cheese and garlic powder in a small bowl, toss well.
3. Cut the jalapeños in half lengthwise. Using a small spoon, scrape out seeds & membranes.
4. Stuff the cheese mixture into the jalapeno halves. Wrap each jalapeno completely with bacon. Secure with toothpicks.
5. Place jalapenos on the grill and grill until cheese mixture is hot and bubbling around the edges, about 30 to 40 minutes.

Nutrition Info:

- Info Per Servings 1.6g Carbs, 5.8g Protein, 15g Fat, 164 Calories

Crispy Chorizo With Cheesy Topping

Servings: 6
Cooking Time: 30 Minutes
Ingredients:

- 7 ounces Spanish chorizo
- 4 ounces cream cheese
- ¼ cup chopped parsley

Directions:

1. Preheat your oven to 325 ºF. Slice the chorizo into 30 slices
2. Line a baking dish with waxed paper. Bake the chorizo for 15 minutes until crispy. Remove from the oven and let cool. Arrange on a serving platter. Top each slice with some cream cheese.
3. Serve sprinkled with chopped parsley.

Nutrition Info:

- Info Per Servings 0g Carbs, 5g Protein, 13g Fat, 172 Calories

Parsnip And Carrot Fries With Aioli

Servings: 4
Cooking Time: 40 Minutes
Ingredients:

- 4 tbsp mayonnaise
- 2 garlic cloves, minced
- Salt and black pepper to taste
- 3 tbsp lemon juice
- Parsnip and Carrots Fries:
- 6 medium parsnips, julienned
- 3 large carrots, julienned
- 2 tbsp olive oil
- 5 tbsp chopped parsley
- Salt and black pepper to taste

Directions:

1. Preheat the oven to 400ºF. Make the aioli by mixing the mayonnaise with garlic, salt, pepper, and lemon juice; then refrigerate for 30 minutes.
2. Spread the parsnip and carrots on a baking sheet. Drizzle with olive oil, sprinkle with salt, and pepper, and rub the seasoning into the veggies. Bake for 35 minutes. Remove and transfer to a plate. Garnish the vegetables with parsley and serve with the chilled aioli.

Nutrition Info:

- Info Per Servings 4.4g Carbs, 2.1g Protein, 4.1g Fat, 205 Calories

Bacon Mashed Cauliflower

Servings: 6
Cooking Time: 40 Minutes
Ingredients:

- 6 slices bacon
- 3 heads cauliflower, leaves removed
- 2 cups water
- 2 tbsp melted butter
- ½ cup buttermilk
- Salt and black pepper to taste
- ¼ cup grated yellow cheddar cheese
- 2 tbsp chopped chives

Directions:

1. Preheat oven to 350ºF. Fry bacon in a heated skillet over medium heat for 5 minutes until crispy. Remove to a paper towel-lined plate, allow to cool, and crumble. Set aside and keep bacon fat.
2. Boil cauli heads in water in a pot over high heat for 7 minutes, until tender. Drain and put in a bowl.
3. Include butter, buttermilk, salt, black pepper, and puree using a hand blender until smooth and creamy. Lightly grease a casserole dish with the bacon fat and spread the mash in it.
4. Sprinkle with cheddar cheese and place under the broiler for 4 minutes on high until the cheese melts. Remove and top with bacon and chopped chives. Serve with pan-seared scallops.

Nutrition Info:

- Info Per Servings 6g Carbs, 14g Protein, 25g Fat, 312 Calories

Middle Eastern Style Tuna Salad

Servings: 6

Cooking Time: 0 Minutes

Ingredients:

- ¼ cup chopped pitted ripe olives
- ¼ cup drained and chopped roasted red peppers
- 2 green onions, sliced
- 2 pcs of 6-oz cans of tuna in water, drained and flaked
- 6 cups salad greens like lettuce
- ¼ cup Mayonnaise

Directions:

1. Except for salad greens, mix all the ingredients in a bowl.
2. Arrange salad greens on the bottom of the bowl and top with tuna mixture.
3. Serve and enjoy.

Nutrition Info:

- Info Per Servings 3g Carbs, 3g Protein, 8g Fat, 92 Calories

Keto "cornbread"

Servings: 8

Cooking Time: 30 Minutes

Ingredients:

- 1 ¼ cups coconut milk
- 4 eggs, beaten
- 4 tbsp baking powder
- ½ cup almond meal
- 3 tablespoons olive oil

Directions:

1. Prepare 8 x 8-inch baking dish or a black iron skillet then add shortening.
2. Put the baking dish or skillet inside the oven on 425oF and leave there for 10 minutes.
3. In a bowl, add coconut milk and eggs then mix well. Stir in the rest of the ingredients.
4. Once all ingredients are mixed, pour the mixture into the heated skillet.
5. Then cook for 15 to 20 minutes in the oven until golden brown.

Nutrition Info:

- Info Per Servings 2.6g Carbs, 5.4g Protein, 18.9g Fat, 196 Calories

Cranberry Sauce Meatballs

Servings: 2

Cooking Time: 25 Mins

Ingredients:

- 1 pound lean ground beef
- 1 egg
- 2 tablespoons water
- 1/2 cup cauliflower rice
- 3 tablespoons minced onion
- 1 can jellied cranberry sauce, keto-friendly
- 3/4 cup chili sauce

Directions:

1. Preheat oven to 350 degrees F.
2. Mix the ground beef, egg, water, cauliflower rice and minced onions together until well combined. Form into small meatballs and place on a rack over a foil-lined baking sheet.
3. Bake the meatballs for 20 to 25 minutes, turning halfway through.
4. Combine sauce ingredients in a large saucepan over low heat, toss with meatballs and allow to simmer on low for 1 hour.
5. Serve and garnish with parsley if desired.

Nutrition Info:

- Info Per Servings 8.6g Carbs, 9.8g Protein, 10.2g Fat, 193 Calories

Keto-approved Trail Mix

Servings: 8

Cooking Time: 3 Minutes

Ingredients:

- ¼ cup salted pumpkin seeds
- ½ cup slivered almonds
- ¾ cup roasted pecan halves
- ¼ cup unsweetened cranberries
- ¾ cup toasted coconut flakes

Directions:

1. In a skillet, place almonds and pecans. Heat for 2-3 minutes and let it cool.
2. Once cooled, in a large resealable plastic bag, combine all ingredients.
3. Seal and shake vigorously to mix.
4. Serve and enjoy.

Nutrition Info:

- Info Per Servings 8.0g Carbs, 4.4g Protein, 14.4g Fat, 184 Calories

Party Bacon And Pistachio Balls

Servings: 8

Cooking Time: 45 Minutes

Ingredients:

- 8 bacon slices, cooked and chopped
- 8 ounces Liverwurst
- ¼ cup chopped pistachios
- 1 tsp Dijon mustard
- 6 ounces cream cheese

Directions:

1. Combine the liverwurst and pistachios in the bowl of your food processor. Pulse until smooth. Whisk the cream cheese and mustard in another bowl. Make 12 balls out of the liverwurst mixture.
2. Make a thin cream cheese layer over. Coat with bacon, arrange on a plate and chill for 30 minutes.

Nutrition Info:

- Info Per Servings 1.5g Carbs, 7g Protein, 12g Fat, 145 Calories

Apricot And Soy Nut Trail Mix

Servings: 20

Cooking Time: 10 Minutes

Ingredients:

- ¼ cup dried apricots, chopped
- 1 cup pumpkin seeds
- ½ cup roasted cashew nuts
- 1 cup roasted, shelled pistachios
- Salt to taste
- 3 tbsp MCT oil or coconut oil

Directions:

1. In a medium mixing bowl, place all ingredients.
2. Thoroughly combine.
3. Bake in the oven for 10 minutes at 3750F.
4. In 20 small zip-top bags, get ¼ cup of the mixture and place in each bag.
5. One zip-top bag is equal to one serving.
6. If properly stored, this can last up to two weeks.

Nutrition Info:

- Info Per Servings 4.6g Carbs, 5.2g Protein, 10.75g Fat, 129 Calories

Sautéed Brussels Sprouts

Servings: 4

Cooking Time: 8 Minutes

Ingredients:

- 2 cups Brussels sprouts, halved
- 1 tablespoon balsamic vinegar
- 4 tablespoons olive oil
- Salt and pepper to taste

Directions:

1. Place a saucepan on medium-high fire and heat oil for a minute.
2. Add all ingredients and sauté for 7 minutes.
3. Season with pepper and salt.
4. Serve and enjoy.

Nutrition Info:

- Info Per Servings 4.6g Carbs, 1.5g Protein, 16.8g Fat, 162 Calories

Choco And Coconut Bars

Servings: 9

Cooking Time: 30 Minutes

Ingredients:

- 1 tbsp Stevia
- ¾ cup shredded coconut, unsweetened
- ½ cup ground nuts (almonds, pecans, or walnuts)
- ¼ cup unsweetened cocoa powder
- 4 tbsp coconut oil

Directions:

1. In a medium bowl, mix shredded coconut, nuts, and cocoa powder.
2. Add Stevia and coconut oil.
3. Mix batter thoroughly.
4. In a 9x9 square inch pan or dish, press the batter and for a 30-minutes place in the freezer.
5. Evenly divide into suggested servings and enjoy.

Nutrition Info:

- Info Per Servings 2.7g Carbs, 1.3g Protein, 9.3g Fat, 99.7 Calories

Baba Ganoush Eggplant Dip

Servings: 4

Cooking Time: 80 Minutes

Ingredients:

- 1 head of garlic, unpeeled
- 1 large eggplant, cut in half lengthwise
- 5 tablespoons olive oil
- Lemon juice to taste
- 2 minced garlic cloves
- What you'll need from the store cupboard:
- Pepper and salt to taste

Directions:

1. With the rack in the middle position, preheat oven to 350°F.
2. Line a baking sheet with parchment paper. Place the eggplant cut side down on the baking sheet.
3. Roast until the flesh is very tender and pulls away easily from the skin, about 1 hour depending on the eggplant's size. Let it cool.
4. Meanwhile, cut the tips off the garlic cloves. Place the cloves in a square of aluminum foil. Fold up the edges of the foil and crimp together to form a tightly sealed packet. Roast alongside the eggplant until tender, about 20 minutes. Let cool.
5. Mash the cloves by pressing with a fork.
6. With a spoon, scoop the flesh from the eggplant and place it in the bowl of a food processor. Add the mashed garlic, oil and lemon juice. Process until smooth. Season with pepper.

Nutrition Info:

- Info Per Servings 10.2g Carbs, 1.6g Protein, 17.8g Fat, 192 Calories

Bacon Jalapeno Poppers

Servings: 8
Cooking Time: 10 Minutes
Ingredients:
- 4-ounce cream cheese
- ¼ cup cheddar cheese, shredded
- 1 teaspoon paprika
- 16 fresh jalapenos, sliced lengthwise and seeded
- 16 strips of uncured bacon, cut into half
- Salt and pepper to taste

Directions:
1. Preheat oven to 400oF.
2. In a mixing bowl, mix the cream cheese, cheddar cheese, salt, and paprika until well-combined.
3. Scoop half a teaspoon onto each half of jalapeno peppers.
4. Use a thin strip of bacon and wrap it around the cheese-filled jalapeno half.
5. Place in a single layer in a lightly greased baking sheet and roast for 10 minutes.
6. Serve and enjoy.

Nutrition Info:
- Info Per Servings 3.2g Carbs, 10.6g Protein, 18.9g Fat, 225 Calories

Pecorino-mushroom Balls

Servings: 4
Cooking Time: 20 Minutes
Ingredients:
- 2 tbsp butter, softened
- 2 garlic cloves, minced
- 2 cups portobello mushrooms, chopped
- 4 tbsp blanched almond flour
- 4 tbsp ground flax seeds
- 4 tbsp hemp seeds
- 4 tbsp sunflower seeds
- 1 tbsp cajun seasonings
- 1 tsp mustard
- 2 eggs, whisked
- ½ cup pecorino cheese

Directions:
1. Set a pan over medium-high heat and warm 1 tablespoon of butter. Add in mushrooms and garlic and sauté until there is no more water in mushrooms.
2. Place in pecorino cheese, almond flour, hemp seeds, mustard, eggs, sunflower seeds, flax seeds, and Cajun seasonings. Create 4 burgers from the mixture.
3. In a pan, warm the remaining butter; fry the burgers for 7 minutes. Flip them over with a wide spatula and cook for 6 more minutes. Serve while warm.

Nutrition Info:
- Info Per Servings 7.7g Carbs, 16.8g Protein, 30g Fat, 370 Calories

Boiled Stuffed Eggs

Servings: 6

Cooking Time: 30 Minutes

Ingredients:

- 6 eggs
- 1 tbsp green tabasco
- ⅓ cup mayonnaise
- Salt to taste

Directions:

1. Place the eggs in a saucepan and cover with salted water. Bring to a boil over medium heat. Boil for 10 minutes. Place the eggs in an ice bath and let cool for 10 minutes.

2. Peel and slice in half lengthwise. Scoop out the yolks to a bowl; mash with a fork. Whisk together the tabasco, mayonnaise, mashed yolks, and salt, in a bowl. Spoon this mixture into egg white.

Nutrition Info:

- Info Per Servings 5g Carbs, 6g Protein, 17g Fat, 178 Calories

Tart Raspberry Crumble Bar

Servings: 9

Cooking Time: 55 Minutes

Ingredients:

- 1/2 cup whole toasted almonds
- 1 cup almond flour
- 1 cup cold, unsalted butter, cut into cubes
- 2 eggs, beaten
- 3-ounce dried raspberries
- 1/4 teaspoon salt
- 3 tbsp MCT or coconut oil.

Directions:

1. In a food processor, pulse almonds until chopped coarsely. Transfer to a bowl.

2. Add almond flour and salt into the food processor and pulse until a bit combined. Add butter, eggs, and MCT oil. Pulse until you have a coarse batter. Evenly divide batter into two bowls.

3. In the first bowl of batter, knead well until it forms a ball. Wrap in cling wrap, flatten a bit and chill for an hour for easy handling.

4. In the second bowl of batter, add the raspberries. In a pinching motion, pinch batter to form clusters of streusel. Set aside.

5. When ready to bake, preheat oven to 375oF and lightly grease an 8x8-inch baking pan with cooking spray.

6. Discard cling wrap and evenly press dough on the bottom of the pan, up to 1-inch up the sides of the pan, making sure that everything is covered in dough.

7. Top with streusel.

8. Pop in the oven and bake until golden brown and berries are bubbly around 45 minutes.

9. Remove from oven and cool for 20 minutes before slicing into 9 equal bars.

10. Serve and enjoy or store in a lidded container for 10-days in the fridge.

Nutrition Info:

- Info Per Servings 3.9g Carbs, 2.8g Protein, 22.9g Fat, 229 Calories

Lemony Fried Artichokes

Servings: 4

Cooking Time: 20 Minutes

Ingredients:

- 12 fresh baby artichokes
- 2 tbsp lemon juice
- 2 tbsp olive oil
- Salt to taste

Directions:

1. Slice the artichokes vertically into narrow wedges. Drain on paper towels before frying.
2. Heat olive oil in a cast-iron skillet over high heat. Fry the artichokes until browned and crispy. Drain excess oil on paper towels. Sprinkle with salt and lemon juice.

Nutrition Info:

- Info Per Servings 2.9g Carbs, 2g Protein, 2.4g Fat, 35 Calories

Mixed Roast Vegetables

Servings: 4

Cooking Time: 40 Minutes

Ingredients:

- 1 large butternut squash, cut into chunks
- ¼ lb shallots, peeled
- 4 rutabagas, cut into chunks
- ¼ lb Brussels sprouts
- 1 sprig rosemary, chopped
- 1 sprig thyme, chopped
- 4 cloves garlic, peeled only
- 3 tbsp olive oil
- Salt and black pepper to taste

Directions:

1. Preheat the oven to 450ºF.
2. Pour the butternut squash, shallots, rutabagas, garlic cloves, and brussels sprouts in a bowl. Season with salt, pepper, olive oil, and toss them. Pour the mixture on a baking sheet and sprinkle with the chopped thyme and rosemary. Roast the vegetables for 15–20 minutes.
3. Once ready, remove and spoon into a serving bowl. Serve with oven roasted chicken thighs.

Nutrition Info:

- Info Per Servings 8g Carbs, 3g Protein, 3g Fat, 65 Calories

Coconut And Chocolate Bars

Servings: 6

Cooking Time: 30 Minutes

Ingredients:

- 1 tbsp Stevia
- ¾ cup shredded coconut, unsweetened
- ½ cup ground nuts (almonds, pecans, or walnuts)
- ¼ cup unsweetened cocoa powder
- 4 tbsp coconut oil
- Done

Directions:

1. In a medium bowl, mix shredded coconut, nuts, and cocoa powder.
2. Add Stevia and coconut oil.
3. Mix batter thoroughly.
4. In a 9x9 square inch pan or dish, press the batter and for a 30-minutes place in the freezer.
5. Serve and enjoy.

Nutrition Info:

- Info Per Servings 2.3g Carbs, 1.6g Protein, 17.8g Fat, 200 Calories

Zucchini And Cheese Gratin

Servings: 8
Cooking Time: 15 Minutes
Ingredients:

- 5 tablespoons butter
- 1 onion, sliced
- ½ cup heavy cream
- 4 cups raw zucchini, sliced
- 1 ½ cups shredded pepper Jack cheese
- Salt and pepper to taste

Directions:

1. Place all ingredients in a mixing bowl and give a good stir to incorporate everything.
2. Pour the mixture in a heat-proof baking dish.
3. Place in a 350F preheated oven and bake for 15 minutes.
4. Serve and enjoy.

Nutrition Info:

- Info Per Servings 5.0g Carbs, 8.0g Protein, 20.0g Fat, 280 Calories

Old Bay Chicken Wings

Servings: 4
Cooking Time: 30 Minutes
Ingredients:

- 3 pounds chicken wings
- ¾ cup almond flour
- 1 tablespoon old bay spices
- 1 teaspoon lemon juice, freshly squeezed
- ½ cup butter
- Salt and pepper to taste

Directions:

1. Preheat oven to 400oF.
2. In a mixing bowl, combine all ingredients except for the butter.
3. Place in an even layer in a baking sheet.
4. Bake for 30 minutes. Halfway through the cooking time, shake the fryer basket for even cooking.
5. Once cooked, drizzle with melted butter.

Nutrition Info:

- Info Per Servings 1.6g Carbs, 52.5g Protein, 59.2g Fat, 700 Calories

Simple Tender Crisp Cauli-bites

Servings: 3
Cooking Time: 10 Minutes
Ingredients:

- 2 cups cauliflower florets
- 2 clove garlic minced
- 4 tablespoons olive oil
- ¼ tsp salt
- ½ tsp pepper

Directions:

1. In a small bowl, mix well olive oil salt, pepper, and garlic.
2. Place cauliflower florets on a baking pan. Drizzle with seasoned oil and toss well to coat.
3. Evenly spread in a single layer and place a pan on the top rack of the oven.
4. Broil on low for 5 minutes. Turnover florets and return to the oven.
5. Continue cooking for another 5 minutes.
6. Serve and enjoy.

Nutrition Info:

- Info Per Servings 4.9g Carbs, 1.7g Protein, 18g Fat, 183 Calories

Squid Salad With Mint, Cucumber & Chili Dressing

Servings: 4

Cooking Time: 30 Minutes

Ingredients:

- 4 medium squid tubes, cut into strips
- ½ cup mint leaves
- 2 medium cucumbers, halved and cut in strips
- ½ cup coriander leaves, reserve the stems
- ½ red onion, finely sliced
- Salt and black pepper to taste
- 1 tsp fish sauce
- 1 red chili, roughly chopped
- 1 tsp swerve
- 1 clove garlic
- 2 limes, juiced
- 1 tbsp chopped coriander
- 1 tsp olive oil

Directions:

1. In a salad bowl, mix mint leaves, cucumber strips, coriander leaves, and red onion. Season with salt, pepper and a little drizzle of olive oil; set aside. In the mortar, pound the coriander stems, red chili, and swerve into a paste using the pestle. Add the fish sauce and lime juice, and mix with the pestle.

2. Heat a skillet over high heat on a stovetop and sear the squid on both sides to lightly brown, about 5 minutes. Pour the squid on the salad and drizzle with the chili dressing. Toss the ingredients with two spoons, garnish with coriander, and serve the salad as a single dish or with some more seafood.

Nutrition Info:

- Info Per Servings 2.1g Carbs, 24.6g Protein, 22.5g Fat, 318 Calories

Sour Cream And Carrot Sticks

Servings: 3

Cooking Time: 0 Minutes

Ingredients:

- 1 sweet onion, peeled and minced
- ½ cup sour cream
- 2 tbsp mayonnaise
- 4 tablespoons olive oil
- 4 stalks celery, cut into 3-inch lengths
- Pepper and salt to taste

Directions:

1. In a bowl, whisk well sour cream and mayonnaise until thoroughly combined.
2. Stir in onion and mix well.
3. Let it sit for an hour in the fridge and serve with celery sticks on the side.

Nutrition Info:

- Info Per Servings 7g Carbs, 3g Protein, 13g Fat, 143 Calories

Pork, Beef & Lamb Recipes

Spiced Pork Roast With Collard Greens

Servings: 4
Cooking Time: 40 Minutes
Ingredients:

- 2 tbsp olive oil
- Salt and black pepper, to taste
- 1 ½ pounds pork loin
- A pinch of dry mustard
- 1 tsp hot red pepper flakes
- ½ tsp ginger, minced
- 1 cup collard greens, chopped
- 2 garlic cloves, minced
- ½ lemon sliced
- ¼ cup water

Directions:

1. Using a bowl, combine the ginger with salt, mustard, and pepper. Add in the meat, toss to coat. Heat the oil in a saucepan over medium-high heat, brown the pork on all sides, for 10 minutes.
2. Transfer to the oven and roast for 1 hour at 390 F. To the saucepan, add collard greens, lemon slices, garlic, and water; cook for 10 minutes. Serve on a platter, sprinkle pan juices on top and enjoy.

Nutrition Info:

- Info Per Servings 3g Carbs, 45g Protein, 23g Fat, 430 Calories

Beef Meatballs

Servings: 5
Cooking Time: 45 Minutes
Ingredients:

- ½ cup pork rinds, crushed
- 1 egg
- Salt and black pepper, to taste
- 1½ pounds ground beef
- 10 ounces canned onion soup
- 1 tbsp almond flour
- ¼ cup free-sugar ketchup
- 3 tsp Worcestershire sauce
- ½ tsp dry mustard
- ¼ cup water

Directions:

1. Using a bowl, combine ⅓ cup of the onion soup with the beef, pepper, pork rinds, egg, and salt. Heat a pan over medium-high heat, shape 12 meatballs from the beef mixture, place them into the pan, and brown on both sides.
2. In a bowl, combine the rest of the soup with the almond flour, dry mustard, ketchup, Worcestershire sauce, and water. Pour this over the beef meatballs, cover the pan, and cook for 20 minutes as you stir occasionally. Split among serving bowls and enjoy.

Nutrition Info:

- Info Per Servings 7g Carbs, 25g Protein, 18g Fat, 332 Calories

Paprika Pork Chops

Servings: 4

Cooking Time: 25 Minutes

Ingredients:

- 4 pork chops
- Salt and black pepper, to taste
- 3 tbsp paprika
- ¾ cup cumin powder
- 1 tsp chili powder

Directions:

1. Using a bowl, combine the paprika with pepper, cumin, salt, and chili. Place in the pork chops and rub them well. Heat a grill over medium temperature, add in the pork chops, cook for 5 minutes, flip, and cook for 5 minutes. Serve with steamed veggies.

Nutrition Info:

- Info Per Servings 4g Carbs, 41.8g Protein, 18.5g Fat, 349 Calories

Creamy Pork Chops

Servings: 3

Cooking Time: 50 Minutes

Ingredients:

- 8 ounces mushrooms, sliced
- 1 tsp garlic powder
- 1 onion, peeled and chopped
- 1 cup heavy cream
- 3 pork chops, boneless
- 1 tsp ground nutmeg
- ¼ cup coconut oil

Directions:

1. Set a pan over medium heat and warm the oil, add in the onions and mushrooms, and cook for 4 minutes. Stir in the pork chops, season with garlic powder, and nutmeg, and sear until browned.

2. Put the pan in the oven at 350ºF, and bake for 30 minutes. Remove pork chops to bowls and maintain warm. Place the pan over medium heat, pour in the heavy cream and vinegar over the mushrooms mixture, and cook for 5 minutes; remove from heat. Sprinkle sauce over pork chops and enjoy.

Nutrition Info:

- Info Per Servings 6.8g Carbs, 42g Protein, 40g Fat, 612 Calories

Spicy Spinach Pinwheel Steaks

Servings: 6

Cooking Time: 42 Minutes

Ingredients:

- Cooking spray
- 1 ½ lb flank steak
- Pink salt and black pepper to season
- 1 cup crumbled feta cheese
- ½ loose cup baby spinach
- 1 jalapeño, chopped
- ¼ cup chopped basil leaves

Directions:

1. Preheat oven to 400ºF and grease a baking sheet with cooking spray.

2. Wrap the steak in plastic wrap, place on a flat surface, and gently run a rolling pin over to flatten. Take off the wraps. Sprinkle with half of the feta cheese, top with spinach, jalapeno, basil leaves, and the remaining cheese. Roll the steak over on the stuffing and secure with toothpicks.

3. Place in the greased baking sheet and cook for 30 minutes, flipping once until nicely browned on the outside and the cheese melted within. Cool for 3 minutes, slice into pinwheels and serve with thyme sautéed mixed veggies.

Nutrition Info:

- Info Per Servings 2g Carbs, 28g Protein, 41g Fat, 490 Calories

Habanero And Beef Balls

Servings: 6
Cooking Time: 45 Minutes
Ingredients:

- 3 garlic cloves, minced
- 1 pound ground beef
- 1 small onion, chopped
- 2 habanero peppers, chopped
- 1 tsp dried thyme
- 2 tsp cilantro
- ½ tsp allspice
- 2 tsp cumin
- A pinch of ground cloves
- Salt and black pepper, to taste
- 2 tbsp butter
- 3 tbsp butter, melted
- 6 ounces cream cheese
- 1 tsp turmeric
- ¼ tsp stevia
- ½ tsp baking powder
- 1½ cups flax meal
- ½ cup coconut flour

Directions:

1. In a blender, mix onion with garlic, habaneros, and ½ cup water. Set a pan over medium heat, add in 2 tbsp butter and cook the beef for 3 minutes. Stir in the onion mixture, and cook for 2 minutes.

2. Stir in cilantro, cloves, salt, cumin, ½ teaspoon turmeric, thyme, allspice, and pepper, and cook for 3 minutes. In a bowl, combine the remaining turmeric, with coconut flour, stevia, flax meal, and baking powder. In a separate bowl, combine the 3 tbsp butter with the cream cheese.

3. Combine the 2 mixtures to obtain a dough. Form 12 balls from this mixture, set them on a parchment paper, and roll each into a circle. Split the beef mix on one-half of the dough circles, cover with the other half, seal edges, and lay on a lined sheet. Bake for 25 minutes in the oven at 350ºF.

Nutrition Info:

- Info Per Servings 8.3g Carbs, 27g Protein, 31g Fat, 455 Calories

Swiss-style Italian Sausage

Servings: 6
Cooking Time: 25 Minutes
Ingredients:

- ¼ cup olive oil
- 2 pounds Italian pork sausage, chopped
- 1 onion, sliced
- 4 sun-dried tomatoes, sliced thin
- Salt and black pepper, to taste
- ½ pound gruyere cheese, grated
- 3 yellow bell peppers, seeded and chopped
- 3 orange bell peppers, seeded and chopped
- A pinch of red pepper flakes
- ½ cup fresh parsley, chopped

Directions:

1. Set a pan over medium-high heat and warm oil, place in the sausage slices, cook each side for 3 minutes, remove to a bowl, and set aside.

2. Stir in the tomatoes, bell peppers, and onion, and cook for 5 minutes. Season with black pepper, pepper flakes, and salt and mix well. Cook for 1 minute, and remove from heat.

3. Lay the sausage slices into a baking dish, place the bell peppers mixture on top, scatter with the gruyere cheese, set in the oven at 340º F, and bake for 10 minutes until the cheese melts. Serve topped with fresh parsley.

Nutrition Info:

- Info Per Servings 7.6g Carbs, 34g Protein, 45g Fat, 567 Calories

Pork Osso Bucco

Servings: 6
Cooking Time: 1 Hour 55 Minutes
Ingredients:

- 4 tbsp butter, softened
- 6 pork shanks
- 2 tbsp olive oil
- 3 cloves garlic, minced
- 1 cup diced tomatoes
- Salt and black pepper to taste
- ½ cup chopped onions
- ½ cup chopped celery
- ½ cup chopped carrots
- 2 cups Cabernet Sauvignon
- 5 cups beef broth
- ½ cup chopped parsley + extra to garnish
- 2 tsp lemon zest

Directions:

1. Melt the butter in a large saucepan over medium heat. Season the pork with salt and pepper and brown it for 12 minutes; remove to a plate.
2. In the same pan, sauté 2 cloves of garlic and onions in the oil, for 3 minutes then return the pork shanks. Stir in the Cabernet, carrots, celery, tomatoes, and beef broth with a season of salt and pepper. Cover the pan and let it simmer on low heat for 1 ½ hours basting the pork every 15 minutes with the sauce.
3. In a bowl, mix the remaining garlic, parsley, and lemon zest to make a gremolata, and stir the mixture into the sauce when it is ready. Turn the heat off and dish the Osso Bucco. Garnish with parsley and serve with a creamy turnip mash.

Nutrition Info:

- Info Per Servings 6.1g Carbs, 34g Protein, 40g Fat, 590 Calories

Cocoa-crusted Pork Tenderloin

Servings: 2
Cooking Time: 25 Minutes
Ingredients:

- 1-pound pork tenderloin, trimmed from fat
- 1 tablespoon cocoa powder
- 1 teaspoon instant coffee powder
- ½ teaspoon ground cinnamon
- ½ teaspoon chili powder
- 1 tablespoon olive oil
- Pepper and salt to taste

Directions:

1. In a bowl, dust the pork tenderloin with cocoa powder, coffee, cinnamon, pepper, salt, and chili powder.
2. In a skillet, heat the oil and sear the meat for 5 minutes on both sides over low to medium flame.
3. Transfer the pork in a baking dish and cook in the oven for 15 minutes in a 350F preheated oven.

Nutrition Info:

- Info Per Servings 2.0g Carbs, 60.0g Protein, 15.0g Fat, 395 Calories

Warm Rump Steak Salad

Servings: 4

Cooking Time: 40 Minutes

Ingredients:

- ½ lb rump steak, excess fat trimmed
- 3 green onions, sliced
- 3 tomatoes, sliced
- 1 cup green beans, steamed and sliced
- 2 kohlrabi, peeled and chopped
- ½ cup water
- 2 cups mixed salad greens
- Salt and black pepper to season
- Salad Dressing
- 2 tsp Dijon mustard
- 1 tsp erythritol
- Salt and black pepper to taste
- 3 tbsp olive oil + extra for drizzling
- 1 tbsp red wine vinegar

Directions:

1. Preheat the oven to 400ºF. Place the kohlrabi on a baking sheet, drizzle with olive oil and bake in the oven for 25 minutes. After cooking, remove, and set aside to cool.

2. In a bowl, mix the Dijon mustard, erythritol, salt, pepper, vinegar, and olive oil. Set aside.

3. Then, preheat a grill pan over high heat while you season the meat with salt and pepper. Place the steak in the pan and brown on both sides for 4 minutes each. Remove to rest on a chopping board for 4 more minutes before slicing thinly.

4. In a shallow salad bowl, add the green onions, tomatoes, green beans, kohlrabi, salad greens, and steak slices. Drizzle the dressing over and toss with two spoons. Serve the rump steak salad warm with chunks of low carb bread.

Nutrition Info:

- Info Per Servings 4g Carbs, 28g Protein, 19g Fat, 325 Calories

Garlic Pork Chops With Mint Pesto

Servings: 4

Cooking Time: 3 Hours 10 Minutes

Ingredients:

- 1 cup parsley
- 1 cup mint
- 1½ onions, chopped
- ⅓ cup pistachios
- 1 tsp lemon zest
- 5 tbsp avocado oil
- Salt, to taste
- 4 pork chops
- 5 garlic cloves, minced
- Juice from 1 lemon

Directions:

1. In a food processor, combine the parsley with avocado oil, mint, pistachios, salt, lemon zest, and 1 onion. Rub the pork with this mixture, place in a bowl, and refrigerate for 1 hour while covered.

2. Remove the chops and set to a baking dish, place in ½ onion, and garlic; sprinkle with lemon juice, and bake for 2 hours in the oven at 250ºF. Split amongst plates and enjoy.

Nutrition Info:

- Info Per Servings 5.5g Carbs, 37g Protein, 40g Fat, 567 Calories

Meatballs With Ranch-buffalo Sauce

Servings: 10

Cooking Time: 30 Minutes

Ingredients:

- 1 packet Ranch dressing dry mix
- 1 bottle red-hot wings buffalo sauce
- 1 bag frozen Rosina Italian Style Meatballs
- 5 tablespoons butter
- 1 cup water
- Pepper and salt to taste

Directions:

1. Add all ingredients in a pot on high fire and bring to a boil.
2. Once boiling, lower fire to a simmer and cook for 25 minutes.
3. Adjust seasoning to taste.
4. Serve and enjoy.

Nutrition Info:

- Info Per Servings 1.2g Carbs, 36.0g Protein, 27.9g Fat, 400 Calories

Sausage Links With Tomatoes & Pesto

Servings: 8

Cooking Time: 15 Minutes

Ingredients:

- 8 pork sausage links, sliced
- 1 lb mixed cherry tomatoes, cut in half
- 4 cups baby spinach
- 1 tbsp olive oil
- 1 pound Monterrey Jack cheese, cubed
- 2 tbsp lemon juice
- 1 cup basil pesto
- Salt and black pepper, to taste

Directions:

1. Set a pan over medium heat and warm oil, place in the sausage slices, and cook each side for 4 minutes. In a salad bowl, combine the spinach with Monterrey jack cheese, salt, pesto, pepper, cherry tomatoes, and lemon juice, and toss well to coat. Toss in the sausage pieces to coat and enjoy.

Nutrition Info:

- Info Per Servings 6.8g Carbs, 18g Protein, 26g Fat, 365 Calories

Classic Italian Bolognese Sauce

Servings: 5

Cooking Time: 35 Minutes

Ingredients:

- 1 pound ground beef
- 2 garlic cloves
- 1 onion, chopped
- 1 tsp oregano
- 1 tsp sage
- 1 tsp marjoram
- 1 tsp rosemary
- 7 oz canned chopped tomatoes
- 1 tbsp olive oil

Directions:

1. Heat olive oil in a saucepan. Add onion and garlic and cook for 3 minutes. Add beef and cook until browned, about 4-5 minutes. Stir in the herbs and tomatoes. Cook for 15 minutes. Serve with zoodles.

Nutrition Info:

- Info Per Servings 5.9g Carbs, 26g Protein, 20g Fat, 318 Calories

Beef Tripe In Vegetable Sauté

Servings: 6

Cooking Time: 27 Minutes + Cooling Time

Ingredients:

- 1 ½ lb beef tripe
- 4 cups buttermilk
- Pink salt to taste
- 2 tsp creole seasoning
- 3 tbsp olive oil
- 2 large onions, sliced
- 3 tomatoes, diced

Directions:

1. Put tripe in a bowl and cover with buttermilk. Refrigerate for 3 hours to extract bitterness and gamey taste. Remove from buttermilk, pat dry with paper towel, and season with salt and creole.

2. Heat 2 tablespoons of oil in a skillet over medium heat and brown the tripe on both sides for 6 minutes in total. Remove and set aside.

3. Add the remaining oil and sauté the onions for 3 minutes until soft. Include the tomatoes and cook for 10 minutes. Pour in a few tablespoons of water if necessary. Put the tripe in the sauce and cook for 3 minutes. Adjust taste with salt and serve with low carb rice.

Nutrition Info:

- Info Per Servings 1g Carbs, 22g Protein, 27g Fat, 342 Calories

Garlicky Pork With Bell Peppers

Servings: 4

Cooking Time: 40 Minutes

Ingredients:

- 3 tbsp butter
- 4 pork steaks, bone-in
- 1 cup chicken stock
- Salt and ground black pepper, to taste
- A pinch of lemon pepper
- 3 tbsp olive oil
- 6 garlic cloves, minced
- 2 tbsp fresh parsley, chopped
- 4 bell peppers, sliced
- 1 lemon, sliced

Directions:

1. Heat a pan with 2 tablespoons oil and 2 tablespoons butter over medium-high heat. Add in the pork steaks, season with pepper and salt, cook until browned; remove to a plate. In the same pan, warm the rest of the oil and butter, add garlic and bell pepper and cook for 4 minutes.

2. Pour the chicken stock, lemon slices, salt, lemon pepper, and black pepper, and cook everything for 5 minutes. Return the pork steaks to the pan and cook for 10 minutes. Split the sauce and steaks among plates and enjoy.

Nutrition Info:

- Info Per Servings 6g Carbs, 40g Protein, 25g Fat, 456 Calories

Bistro Beef Tenderloin

Servings: 7
Cooking Time: 45 Minutes
Ingredients:

- 1 3-pound beef tenderloin, trimmed of fat
- 2/3 cup chopped mixed herbs
- 2 tablespoons Dijon mustard
- 5 tablespoons extra virgin olive oil
- ½ teaspoon ground black pepper
- ½ tsp salt

Directions:

1. Preheat the oven to 400F.
2. Secure the beef tenderloin with a string in three places so that it does not flatten while roasting.
3. Place the beef tenderloin in a dish and rub onto the meat the olive oil, black pepper, salt, and mixed herb.
4. Place on a roasting pan and cook in the oven for 45 minutes.
5. Roast until the thermometer inserted into the thickest part of the meat until it registers 1400F for medium rare.
6. Place the tenderloin on a chopping board and remove the string. Slice into 1-inch thick slices and brush with Dijon mustard.

Nutrition Info:

- Info Per Servings 0.6g Carbs, 59.0g Protein, 22.0g Fat, 440 Calories

Hot Pork With Dill Pickles

Servings: 4
Cooking Time: 20 Minutes
Ingredients:

- ¼ cup lime juice
- 4 pork chops
- 1 tbsp coconut oil, melted
- 2 garlic cloves, minced
- 1 tbsp chili powder
- 1 tsp ground cinnamon
- 2 tsp cumin
- Salt and black pepper, to taste
- ½ tsp hot pepper sauce
- 4 dill pickles, cut into spears and squeezed

Directions:

1. Using a bowl, combine the lime juice with oil, cumin, salt, hot pepper sauce, pepper, cinnamon, garlic, and chili powder. Place in the pork chops, toss to coat, and refrigerate for 4 hours.
2. Arrange the pork on a preheated grill over medium heat, cook for 7 minutes, turn, add in the dill pickles, and cook for another 7 minutes. Split among serving plates and enjoy.

Nutrition Info:

- Info Per Servings 2.3g Carbs, 36g Protein, 18g Fat, 315 Calories

Beef Brisket In Mustard Sauce

Servings: 7
Cooking Time: 60 Minutes
Ingredients:

- 2 ½ pounds beef brisket, cut into 2-inch cubes
- ½ cup onion, chopped
- 1 tablespoon prepared mustard
- ½ cup olive oil
- Salt and pepper to taste
- 1 cup water

Directions:

1. Place all ingredients in a heavy-bottomed pot on high fire and bring to a boil.
2. Once boiling, lower fire to a simmer.
3. Simmer for 60 minutes.
4. Serve and enjoy.

Nutrition Info:

- Info Per Servings 1.7g Carbs, 29.4g Protein, 39.2g Fat, 477 Calories

Parsley Beef Burgers

Servings: 6
Cooking Time: 25 Minutes
Ingredients:
- 2 pounds ground beef
- 1 tbsp onion flakes
- ¾ almond flour
- ¼ cup beef broth
- 1 tbsp chopped parsley
- 1 tbsp Worcestershire sauce

Directions:
1. Combine all ingredients in a bowl. Mix well with your hands and make 6 patties out of the mixture. Arrange on a lined baking sheet. Bake at 370ºF, for about 18 minutes, until nice and crispy.

Nutrition Info:
- Info Per Servings 2.5g Carbs, 27g Protein, 28g Fat, 354 Calories

Balsamic Grilled Pork Chops

Servings: 6
Cooking Time: 2 Hours 20 Minutes
Ingredients:
- 6 pork loin chops, boneless
- 2 tbsp erythritol
- ¼ cup balsamic vinegar
- 3 cloves garlic, minced
- ¼ cup olive oil
- ⅓ tsp salt
- Black pepper to taste

Directions:
1. Put the pork in a plastic bag. In a bowl, mix the erythritol, balsamic vinegar, garlic, olive oil, salt, pepper, and pour the sauce over the pork. Seal the bag, shake it, and place in the refrigerator.
2. Marinate the pork for 1 to 2 hours. Preheat the grill on medium-high heat, remove the pork when ready, and grill covered for 10 to 12 minutes on each side. Remove the pork chops, let them sit for 4 minutes, and serve with a syrupy parsnip sauté.

Nutrition Info:
- Info Per Servings 1.5g Carbs, 38.1g Protein, 26.8g Fat, 418 Calories

Charred Tenderloin With Lemon Chimichurri

Servings: 4

Cooking Time: 64 Minutes

Ingredients:

- Lemon Chimichurri
- 1 lemon, juiced
- ¼ cup chopped mint leaves
- ¼ cup chopped oregano leaves
- 2 cloves garlic, minced
- ¼ cup olive oil
- Salt to taste
- Pork
- 1 pork tenderloin
- Salt and black pepper to season
- Olive oil for rubbing

Directions:

1. Make the lemon chimichurri to have the flavors incorporate while the pork cooks.
2. In a bowl, mix the mint, oregano, and garlic. Then, add the lemon juice, olive oil, and salt, and combine well. Set the sauce aside at room temperature.
3. Preheat the charcoal grill to 450ºF in medium-high heat creating a direct heat area and indirect heat area. Rub the pork with olive oil, season with salt and pepper. Place the meat over direct heat and sear for 3 minutes on each side, after which, move to the indirect heat area.
4. Close the lid and cook for 25 minutes on one side, then open, turn the meat, and grill closed for 20 minutes on the other side. Remove the pork from the grill and let it sit for 5 minutes before slicing. Spoon lemon chimichurri over the pork and serve with a fresh salad.

Nutrition Info:

- Info Per Servings 2.1g Carbs, 28g Protein, 18g Fat, 388 Calories

Easy Thai 5-spice Pork Stew

Servings: 9

Cooking Time: 40 Minutes

Ingredients:

- 2 lb. pork butt, cut into chunks
- 2 tbsp. 5-spice powder
- 2 cups coconut milk, freshly squeezed
- 1 ½ tbsp sliced ginger
- 1 cup chopped cilantro
- 1 tsp oil
- Salt and pepper to taste
- ½ cup water

Directions:

1. Place a heavy-bottomed pot on medium-high fire and heat for 2 minutes. Add oil and heat for a minute.
2. Stir in pork chunks and cook for 3 minutes per side.
3. Add ginger, cilantro, pepper, and salt. Sauté for 2 minutes.
4. Add water and deglaze the pot. Stir in 5-spice powder.
5. Cover and simmer for 20 minutes.
6. Stir in coconut milk. Cover and cook for another 10 minutes.
7. Adjust seasoning if needed.
8. Serve and enjoy.

Nutrition Info:

- Info Per Servings 4.4g Carbs, 39.8g Protein, 30.5g Fat, 398 Calories

Adobo Beef Fajitas

Servings: 4
Cooking Time: 35 Minutes
Ingredients:

- 2 lb skirt steak, cut in halves
- 2 tbsp Adobo seasoning
- Pink salt to taste
- 2 tbsp olive oil
- 2 large white onion, chopped
- 1 cup sliced mixed bell peppers, chopped
- 12 low carb tortillas

Directions:

1. Season the steak with adobo and marinate in the fridge for one hour.
2. Preheat grill to 425°F and cook steak for 6 minutes on each side, flipping once until lightly browned. Remove from heat and wrap in foil and let sit for 10 minutes. This allows the meat to cook in its heat for a few more minutes before slicing.
3. Heat the olive oil in a skillet over medium heat and sauté the onion and bell peppers for 5 minutes or until soft. Cut steak against the grain into strips and share on the tortillas. Top with the veggies and serve with guacamole.

Nutrition Info:

- Info Per Servings 5g Carbs, 18g Protein, 25g Fat, 348 Calories

Beef With Dilled Yogurt

Servings: 6
Cooking Time: 25 Minutes
Ingredients:

- ¼ cup almond milk
- 2 pounds ground beef
- 1 onion, grated
- 5 zero carb bread slices, torn
- 1 egg, whisked
- ¼ cup fresh parsley, chopped
- Salt and black pepper, to taste
- 2 garlic cloves, minced
- ¼ cup fresh mint, chopped
- 2 ½ tsp dried oregano
- ¼ cup olive oil
- 1 cup cherry tomatoes, halved
- 1 cucumber, sliced
- 1 cup baby spinach
- 1½ tbsp lemon juice
- 1 cup dilled Greek yogurt

Directions:

1. Place the torn bread in a bowl, add in the milk, and set aside for 3 minutes. Squeeze the bread, chop, and place into a bowl. Stir in the beef, salt, mint, onion, parsley, pepper, egg, oregano, and garlic.
2. Form balls out of this mixture and place on a working surface. Set a pan over medium heat and warm half of the oil; fry the meatballs for 8 minutes. Flip occasionally, and set aside in a tray.
3. In a salad plate, combine the spinach with the cherry tomatoes and cucumber. Mix in the remaining oil, lemon juice, black pepper, and salt. Spread dilled yogurt over, and top with meatballs to serve.

Nutrition Info:

- Info Per Servings 8.3g Carbs, 27g Protein, 22.4g Fat, 408 Calories

Beef Bourguignon

Servings: 4

Cooking Time: 60 Minutes + Marinated Time

Ingredients:

- 3 tbsp coconut oil
- 1 tbsp dried parsley flakes
- 1 cup red wine
- 1 tsp dried thyme
- Salt and black pepper, to taste
- 1 bay leaf
- ⅓ cup coconut flour
- 2 lb beef, cubed
- 12 small white onions
- 4 pancetta slices, chopped
- 2 garlic cloves, minced
- ½ lb mushrooms, chopped

Directions:

1. In a bowl, combine the wine with bay leaf, olive oil, thyme, pepper, parsley, salt, and the beef cubes; set aside for 3 hours. Drain the meat, and reserve the marinade. Toss the flour over the meat to coat.

2. Heat a pan over medium-high heat, stir in the pancetta, and cook until slightly browned. Place in the onions and garlic, and cook for 3 minutes. Stir-fry in the meat and mushrooms for 4-5 minutes.

3. Pour in the marinade and 1 cup of water; cover and cook for 50 minutes. Season to taste and serve.

Nutrition Info:

- Info Per Servings 7g Carbs, 45g Protein, 26g Fat, 435 Calories

Poultry Recipes

Easy Chicken Vindaloo

Servings: 5
Cooking Time: 30 Minutes
Ingredients:

- 1 lb. chicken thighs, skin and bones not removed
- 2 tbsp. garam masala
- 6 whole red dried chilies
- 1 onion, sliced
- 5 cloves of garlic, crushed
- Pepper and salt to taste
- 1 tsp oil
- 1 cup water

Directions:

1. On high fire, heat a saucepan for 2 minutes. Add oil to the pan and swirl to coat bottom and sides. Heat oil for a minute.
2. Add chicken with skin side touching pan and sear for 5 minutes. Turn chicken over and sear the other side for 3 minutes. Transfer chicken to a plate.
3. In the same pan, sauté garlic for a minute. Add onion and sauté for 3 minutes. Stir in garam masala and chilies.
4. Return chicken to the pot and mix well. Add water and season with pepper and salt.
5. Cover and lower fire to simmer and cook for 15 minutes.
6. Serve and enjoy.

Nutrition Info:

- Info Per Servings 1.4g Carbs, 15.2g Protein, 15.1g Fat, 206 Calories

Pacific Chicken

Servings: 6
Cooking Time: 50 Minutes
Ingredients:

- 4 chicken breasts
- Salt and black pepper, to taste
- ½ cup mayonnaise
- 3 tbsp Dijon mustard
- 1 tsp xylitol
- ¾ cup pork rinds
- ¾ cup grated Grana-Padano cheese
- 2 tsp garlic powder
- 1 tsp onion powder
- ¼ tsp salt
- ¼ tsp black pepper
- 8 pieces ham, sliced
- 4 slices gruyere cheese

Directions:

1. Set an oven to 350ºF and grease a baking dish. Using a small bowl, place in the pork rinds and crush. Add chicken to a plate and season well.
2. In a separate bowl, mix mustard, mayonnaise, and xylitol. Take about ¼ of this mixture and spread over the chicken. Preserve the rest. Take ½ pork rinds, seasonings, most of Grana-Padano cheese, and place to the bottom of the baking dish. Add the chicken to the top.
3. Cover the chicken with the remaining Grana-Padano, pork rinds, and seasonings. Place in the oven for about 40 minutes until the chicken is cooked completely. Take out from the oven and top with gruyere cheese and ham. Place back in the oven and cook until golden brown.

Nutrition Info:

- Info Per Servings 2.6g Carbs, 33g Protein, 31g Fat, 465 Calories

Easy Bbq Chicken And Cheese

Servings: 4

Cooking Time: 40 Minutes

Ingredients:

- 1-pound chicken tenders, boneless
- ½ cup commercial BBQ sauce, keto-friendly
- 1 teaspoon liquid smoke
- 1 cup mozzarella cheese, grated
- ½ pound bacon, fried and crumbled
- Pepper and salt to taste

Directions:

1. With paper towels, dry chicken tenders. Season with pepper and salt.
2. Place chicken tenders on an oven-safe dish.
3. Whisk well BBQ sauce and liquid smoke in a bowl and pour over chicken tenders. Coat well in the sauce.
4. Bake in a preheated 400oF oven for 30 minutes.
5. Remove from oven, turnover chicken tenders, sprinkle cheese on top.
6. Return to the oven and continue baking for 10 minutes more.
7. Serve and enjoy with a sprinkle of bacon bits.

Nutrition Info:

- Info Per Servings 6.7g Carbs, 34.6g Protein, 31.5g Fat, 351 Calories

Spinach Artichoke Heart Chicken

Servings: 4

Cooking Time: 30 Minutes

Ingredients:

- 4 chicken breasts
- 1 package frozen spinach
- 1 package cream cheese, softened
- ½ can quartered artichoke hearts, drained and chopped
- ¼ cup. shredded Parmesan cheese
- ¼ cup. mayonnaise
- 2 tbsp. olive oil
- 2 tbsps. grated mozzarella cheese
- ½ teaspoon. garlic powder
- Salt to taste

Directions:

1. Place the spinach in a bowl and microwave for 2 to 3 minutes. Let chill and drain.
2. Stir in cream cheese, artichoke hearts, Parmesan cheese, mayonnaise, garlic powder, and salt, whisk together. Cut chicken breasts to an even thickness. Spread salt and pepper over chicken breasts per side.
3. Preheat oven to 375 degrees F.
4. In a large skillet over medium-high, heat olive oil for 2 to 3 minutes. Lay chicken breasts in a large baking dish, pour spinach-artichoke mixture over chicken breasts. Place in the oven and bake at least 165 degrees F.
5. Sprinkle with mozzarella cheese and bake for 1 to 2 minutes more. Serve and enjoy.

Nutrition Info:

- Info Per Servings 5.4g Carbs, 56g Protein, 33.3g Fat, 554 Calories

Paprika Chicken With Cream Sauce

Servings: 4

Cooking Time: 50 Minutes

Ingredients:

- 1 pound chicken thighs
- Salt and black pepper, to taste
- 1 tsp onion powder
- ¼ cup heavy cream
- 2 tbsp butter
- 2 tbsp sweet paprika

Directions:

1. Using a bowl, combine the paprika with onion powder, pepper, and salt. Season chicken pieces with this mixture and lay on a lined baking sheet; bake for 40 minutes in the oven at 400ºF. Split the chicken in serving plates, and set aside.

2. Add the cooking juices to a skillet over medium heat, and mix with the heavy cream and butter. Cook for 5-6 minutes until the sauce is thickened. Sprinkle the sauce over the chicken and serve.

Nutrition Info:

- Info Per Servings 2.6g Carbs, 31.3g Protein, 33g Fat, 381 Calories

Avocado Cheese Pepper Chicken

Servings: 5

Cooking Time: 20 Minutes

Ingredients:

- ¼ tsp. cayenne pepper
- 1½ cup. cooked and shredded chicken
- 2 tbsps. cream cheese
- 2 tbsps. lemon juice
- 2 large avocados, diced
- Black pepper and salt to taste
- ¼ cup. mayonnaise
- 1 tsp. dried thyme
- ½ tsp. onion powder
- ½ tsp. garlic powder

Directions:

1. Remove the insides of your avocado halves and set them in a bowl.
2. Stir all ingredients to avocado flesh.
3. Fill avocados with chicken mix.
4. Serve and enjoy.

Nutrition Info:

- Info Per Servings 5g Carbs, 24g Protein, 40g Fat, 476 Calories

Buttered Duck Breast

Servings: 1

Cooking Time: 30 Minutes

Ingredients:

- 1 medium duck breast, skin scored
- 1 tbsp heavy cream
- 2 tbsp butter
- Salt and black pepper, to taste
- 1 cup kale
- ¼ tsp fresh sage

Directions:

1. Set the pan over medium-high heat and warm half of the butter. Place in sage and heavy cream, and cook for 2 minutes. Set another pan over medium-high heat. Place in the remaining butter and duck breast as the skin side faces down, cook for 4 minutes, flip, and cook for 3 more minutes.

2. Place the kale to the pan containing the sauce, cook for 1 minute. Set the duck breast on a flat surface and slice. Arrange the duck slices on a platter and drizzle over the sauce.

Nutrition Info:

- Info Per Servings 2g Carbs, 35g Protein, 46g Fat, 547 Calories

Zesty Grilled Chicken

Servings: 8

Cooking Time: 35 Minutes

Ingredients:

- 2½ pounds chicken thighs and drumsticks
- 1 tbsp coconut aminos
- 1 tbsp apple cider vinegar
- A pinch of red pepper flakes
- Salt and black pepper, to taste
- ½ tsp ground ginger
- ⅓ cup butter
- 1 garlic clove, minced
- 1 tsp lime zest
- ½ cup warm water

Directions:

1. In a blender, combine the butter with water, salt, ginger, vinegar, garlic, pepper, lime zest, aminos, and pepper flakes. Pat the chicken pieces dry, lay on a pan, and top with the zesty marinade.
2. Toss to coat and refrigerate for 1 hour. Set the chicken pieces skin side down on a preheated grill over medium-high heat, cook for 10 minutes, turn, brush with some marinade, and cook for 10 minutes. Split among serving plates and enjoy.

Nutrition Info:

- Info Per Servings 3g Carbs, 42g Protein, 12g Fat, 375 Calories

Chicken Chipotle

Servings: 8

Cooking Time: 25 Minutes

Ingredients:

- 4 tablespoons McCormick grill mates' chipotle
- Roasted garlic seasoning
- 8 garlic cloves peeled and crushed
- 5-pounds whole chicken
- ½ cup water

Directions:

1. Add all ingredients in a pot on high fire and bring it to a boil.
2. Once boiling, lower fire to a simmer and cook for 25 minutes.
3. Adjust seasoning to taste.
4. Serve and enjoy.

Nutrition Info:

- Info Per Servings 5.7g Carbs, 52.0g Protein, 42.5g Fat, 613 Calories

Turkey & Leek Soup

Servings: 4

Cooking Time: 45 Minutes

Ingredients:

- 3 celery stalks, chopped
- 2 leeks, chopped
- 1 tbsp butter
- 6 cups chicken stock
- Salt and ground black pepper, to taste
- ¼ cup fresh parsley, chopped
- 3 cups zoodles
- 3 cups turkey meat, cooked and chopped

Directions:

1. Set a pot over medium-high heat, stir in leeks and celery and cook for 5 minutes. Place in the parsley, turkey meat, pepper, salt, and stock, and cook for 20 minutes. Stir in the zoodles, and cook turkey soup for 5 minutes. Serve in bowls and enjoy.

Nutrition Info:

- Info Per Servings 3g Carbs, 15g Protein, 11g Fat, 305 Calories

Cheesy Chicken Bake With Zucchini

Servings: 12
Cooking Time: 45 Minutes
Ingredients:

- 2 lb chicken breasts, cubed
- 1 tbsp butter
- 1 cup green bell peppers, sliced
- 1 cup yellow onions, sliced
- 1 zucchini, sliced
- 2 garlic cloves, divided
- 2 tsp Italian seasoning
- ½ tsp salt
- ½ tsp black pepper
- 8 oz cream cheese, softened
- ½ cup mayonnaise
- 2 tbsp Worcestershire sauce (sugar-free)
- 2 cups cheddar cheese, shredded

Directions:

1. Set oven to 370ºF and grease and line a baking dish.
2. Set a pan over medium-high heat. Place in the butter and let melt, then add in the chicken.
3. Cook until browned. Place in onions, zucchini, black pepper, garlic, peppers, salt, and 1 tsp of Italian seasonings. Cook until tender. Set aside.
4. In a bowl, mix cream cheese, garlic, cheddar cheese, remaining seasoning, mayonnaise, and Worcestershire sauce. Stir in meat. Place the mixture into the prepared baking dish then set into the oven. Cook until browned for 30 minutes.

Nutrition Info:

- Info Per Servings 4.5g Carbs, 21g Protein, 37g Fat, 489 Calories

Chicken Paella With Chorizo

Servings: 6
Cooking Time: 63 Minutes
Ingredients:

- 18 chicken drumsticks
- 12 oz chorizo, chopped
- 1 white onion, chopped
- 4 oz jarred piquillo peppers, finely diced
- 2 tbsp olive oil
- ½ cup chopped parsley
- 1 tsp smoked paprika
- 2 tbsp tomato puree
- ½ cup white wine
- 1 cup chicken broth
- 2 cups cauli rice
- 1 cup chopped green beans
- 1 lemon, cut in wedges
- Salt and pepper, to taste

Directions:

1. Preheat the oven to 350ºF.
2. Heat the olive oil in a cast iron pan over medium heat, meanwhile season the chicken with salt and pepper, and fry in the hot oil on both sides for 10 minutes to lightly brown. After, remove onto a plate with a perforated spoon.
3. Then, add the chorizo and onion to the hot oil, and sauté for 4 minutes. Include the tomato puree, piquillo peppers, and paprika and let simmer for 2 minutes. Add the broth, and bring the ingredients to boil for 6 minutes until slightly reduced.
4. Stir in the cauli rice, white wine, green beans, half of the parsley, and lay the chicken on top. Transfer the pan to the oven and continue cooking for 20-25 minutes. Let the paella sit to cool for 10 minutes before serving garnished with the remaining parsley and lemon wedges.

Nutrition Info:

- Info Per Servings 3g Carbs, 22g Protein, 28g Fat, 440 Calories

Cilantro Chicken Breasts With Mayo-avocado Sauce

Servings: 4

Cooking Time: 22 Minutes

Ingredients:

- For the Sauce
- 1 avocado, pitted
- ½ cup mayonnaise
- Salt to taste
- For the Chicken
- 3 tbsp ghee
- 4 chicken breasts
- Pink salt and black pepper to taste
- 1 cup chopped cilantro leaves
- ½ cup chicken broth

Directions:

1. Spoon the avocado, mayonnaise, and salt into a small food processor and puree until smooth sauce is derived. Adjust taste with salt as desired.

2. Pour sauce into a jar and refrigerate while you make the chicken.

3. Melt ghee in a large skillet, season chicken with salt and black pepper and fry for 4 minutes on each side to golden brown. Remove chicken to a plate.

4. Pour the broth in the same skillet and add the cilantro. Bring to simmer covered for 3 minutes and add the chicken. Cover and cook on low heat for 5 minutes until liquid has reduced and chicken is fragrant. Dish chicken only into serving plates and spoon the mayo-avocado sauce over.

Nutrition Info:

- Info Per Servings 4g Carbs, 24g Protein, 32g Fat, 398 Calories

Chicken Country Style

Servings: 4

Cooking Time: 25 Minutes

Ingredients:

- 3 tablespoons butter
- 1 packet dry Lipton's onion soup mix
- 1 can Campbell's chicken gravy
- 4 skinless and boneless chicken breasts
- 1/3 teaspoon pepper
- 1 cup water

Directions:

1. Add all ingredients in a pot on high fire and bring it to a boil.

2. Once boiling, lower fire to a simmer and cook for 25 minutes.

3. Adjust seasoning to taste.

4. Serve and enjoy.

Nutrition Info:

- Info Per Servings 6.8g Carbs, 53.7g Protein, 16.9g Fat, 380 Calories

Duck & Vegetable Casserole

Servings: 2

Cooking Time: 20 Minutes

Ingredients:

- 2 duck breasts, skin on and sliced
- 2 zucchinis, sliced
- 1 tbsp coconut oil
- 1 green onion bunch, chopped
- 1 carrot, chopped
- 2 green bell peppers, seeded and chopped
- Salt and ground black pepper, to taste

Directions:

1. Set a pan over medium-high heat and warm oil, stir in the green onions, and cook for 2 minutes. Place in the zucchini, bell peppers, pepper, salt, and carrot, and cook for 10 minutes.

2. Set another pan over medium-high heat, add in duck slices and cook each side for 3 minutes. Pour the mixture into the vegetable pan. Cook for 3 minutes. Set in bowls and enjoy.

Nutrition Info:

- Info Per Servings 8g Carbs, 53g Protein, 21g Fat, 433 Calories

Tender Turkey Breast

Servings: 12

Cooking Time: 25 Minutes

Ingredients:

- 4 peeled garlic cloves
- 4 fresh rosemary sprigs
- 1 bone-in turkey breast
- 5 tablespoons olive oil
- ½ teaspoon coarsely ground pepper
- ¼ teaspoon salt
- ½ cup water

Directions:

1. Add all ingredients in a pot on high fire and bring it to a boil.
2. Once boiling, lower fire to a simmer and cook for 20 minutes.
3. Adjust seasoning to taste.
4. Serve and enjoy.

Nutrition Info:

- Info Per Servings 0.8g Carbs, 35.8g Protein, 22.7g Fat, 390 Calories

One Pot Chicken Alfredo

Servings: 4

Cooking Time: 20 Minutes

Ingredients:

- 1-pound cooked chicken breasts, chopped
- 1 jar Prego Alfredo Sauce
- ¼ cup mozzarella cheese
- ½ cup bacon bits, fried and crumbled
- Pepper and salt to taste
- 2 tbsp water

Directions:

1. Add all ingredients in a pot.
2. Close the lid and bring to a boil over medium flame.
3. Allow simmering for 20 minutes.
4. Serve and enjoy.

Nutrition Info:

- Info Per Servings 6.5g Carbs, 53.4g Protein, 64.5g Fat, 899 Calories

Chicken Garam Masala

Servings: 4
Cooking Time: 45 Minutes
Ingredients:

- 1 lb chicken breasts, sliced lengthwise
- 2 tbsp butter
- 1 tbsp olive oil
- 1 yellow bell pepper, finely chopped
- 1 ¼ cups heavy whipping cream
- 1 tbsp fresh cilantro, finely chopped
- Salt and pepper, to taste
- For the garam masala
- 1 tsp ground cumin
- 2 tsp ground coriander
- 1 tsp ground cardamom
- 1 tsp turmeric
- 1 tsp ginger
- 1 tsp paprika
- 1 tsp cayenne, ground
- 1 pinch ground nutmeg

Directions:

1. Set your oven to 400ºF. In a bowl, mix the garam masala spices. Coat the chicken with half of the masala mixture. Heat the olive oil and butter in a frying pan over medium-high heat, and brown the chicken for 3-5 minutes per side. Transfer to a baking dish.
2. To the remaining masala, add heavy cream and bell pepper. Season with salt and pepper and pour over the chicken. Bake in the oven for 20 minutes until the mixture starts to bubble. Garnish with chopped cilantro to serve.

Nutrition Info:

- Info Per Servings 5g Carbs, 33g Protein, 50g Fat, 564 Calories

Chicken Breasts With Cheddar & Pepperoni

Servings: 4
Cooking Time: 40 Minutes
Ingredients:

- 12 oz canned tomato sauce
- 1 tbsp olive oil
- 4 chicken breast halves, skinless and boneless
- Salt and ground black pepper, to taste
- 1 tsp dried oregano
- 4 oz cheddar cheese, sliced
- 1 tsp garlic powder
- 2 oz pepperoni, sliced

Directions:

1. Preheat your oven to 390ºF. Using a bowl, combine chicken with oregano, salt, garlic, and pepper.
2. Heat a pan with the olive oil over medium-high heat, add in the chicken, cook each side for 2 minutes, and remove to a baking dish. Top with the cheddar cheese slices spread the sauce, then cover with pepperoni slices. Bake for 30 minutes. Serve warm garnished with fresh oregano if desired

Nutrition Info:

- Info Per Servings 4.5g Carbs, 32g Protein, 21g Fat, 387 Calories

Yummy Chicken Queso

Servings: 4

Cooking Time: 25 Minutes

Ingredients:

- ½ teaspoon garlic salt
- 4-ounce can diced drained green chiles
- 10-ounce can mild rotel drained
- ¾ cup medium queso dip
- 4 boneless skinless boneless fresh or thawed chicken breasts
- 5 tablespoons olive oil
- 1 cup water

Directions:

1. Add all ingredients in a pot on high fire and bring it to a boil.
2. Once boiling, lower fire to a simmer and cook for 20 minutes. Stir frequently.
3. Adjust seasoning to taste.
4. Serve and enjoy.

Nutrition Info:

- Info Per Servings 7.2g Carbs, 56.6g Protein, 21.7g Fat, 500 Calories

Roast Chicken With Herb Stuffing

Servings: 8

Cooking Time: 120 Minutes

Ingredients:

- 5-pound whole chicken
- 1 bunch oregano
- 1 bunch thyme
- 1 tbsp marjoram
- 1 tbsp parsley
- 1 tbsp olive oil
- 2 pounds Brussels sprouts
- 1 lemon
- 4 tbsp butter

Directions:

1. Preheat your oven to 450ºF.
2. Stuff the chicken with oregano, thyme, and lemon. Make sure the wings are tucked over and behind.
3. Roast for 15 minutes. Reduce the heat to 325ºF and cook for 40 minutes. Spread the butter over the chicken, and sprinkle parsley and marjoram. Add the brussels sprouts. Return to the oven and bake for 40 more minutes. Let sit for 10 minutes before carving.

Nutrition Info:

- Info Per Servings 5.1g Carbs, 30g Protein, 32g Fat, 432 Calories

Chicken Curry

Servings: 6

Cooking Time: 30 Minutes

Ingredients:

- 1 ½ lb. boneless chicken breasts
- 2 tbsp. curry powder
- 2 cups chopped tomatoes
- 2 cups coconut milk, freshly squeezed
- 1 thumb-size ginger, peeled and sliced
- Pepper and salt to taste
- 2 tsp oil, divided

Directions:

1. On high fire, heat a saucepan for 2 minutes. Add 1 tsp oil to the pan and swirl to coat bottom and sides. Heat oil for a minute.
2. Sear chicken breasts for 4 minutes per side. Transfer to a chopping board and chop into bite-sized pieces.
3. Meanwhile, in the same pan, add remaining oil and heat for a minute. Add ginger sauté for a minute. Stir in tomatoes and curry powder. Crumble and wilt tomatoes for 5 minutes.
4. Add chopped chicken and continue sautéing for 7 minutes.
5. Deglaze the pot with 1 cup of coconut milk. Season with pepper and salt. Cover and simmer for 15 minutes.
6. Stir in remaining coconut milk and cook until heated through, around 3 minutes.

Nutrition Info:

- Info Per Servings 7.4g Carbs, 28.1g Protein, 22.4g Fat, 336 Calories

Cheese Stuffed Chicken Breasts With Spinach

Servings: 4

Cooking Time: 50 Minutes

Ingredients:

- 4 chicken breasts, boneless and skinless
- ½ cup mozzarella cheese
- ⅓ cup Parmesan cheese
- 6 ounces cream cheese
- 2 cups spinach, chopped
- A pinch of nutmeg
- ½ tsp minced garlic
- Breading:
- 2 eggs
- ⅓ cup almond flour
- 2 tbsp olive oil
- ½ tsp parsley
- ⅓ cup Parmesan cheese
- A pinch of onion powder

Directions:

1. Pound the chicken until it doubles in size. Mix the cream cheese, spinach, mozzarella, nutmeg, salt, pepper, and parmesan in a bowl. Divide the mixture between the chicken breasts and spread it out evenly. Wrap the chicken in a plastic wrap. Refrigerate for 15 minutes.
2. Heat the oil in a pan and preheat the oven to 370ºF. Beat the eggs and combine all other breading ingredients in a bowl. Dip the chicken in egg first, then in the breading mixture. Cook in the pan until browned. Place on a lined baking sheet and bake for 20 minutes.

Nutrition Info:

- Info Per Servings 3.5g Carbs, 38g Protein, 36g Fat, 491 Calories

Red Wine Chicken

Servings: 4
Cooking Time: 30 Minutes
Ingredients:

- 3 tbsp coconut oil
- 2 lb chicken breast halves, skinless and boneless
- 3 garlic cloves, minced
- Salt and black pepper, to taste
- 1 cup chicken stock
- 3 tbsp stevia
- ½ cup red wine
- 2 tomatoes, sliced
- 6 mozzarella slices
- Fresh basil, chopped, for serving

Directions:

1. Set a pan over medium-high heat and warm oil, add the chicken, season with pepper and salt, cook until brown. Stir in the stevia, garlic, stock, and red wine, and cook for 10 minutes.
2. Remove to a lined baking sheet and arrange mozzarella cheese slices on top. Broil in the oven over medium heat until cheese melts and lay tomato slices over chicken pieces.
3. Sprinkle with chopped basil to serve.

Nutrition Info:

- Info Per Servings 4g Carbs, 27g Protein, 12g Fat, 314 Calories

Oven-baked Skillet Lemon Chicken

Servings: 4
Cooking Time: 60 Minutes
Ingredients:

- 6 small chicken thighs
- 1 medium onion
- 1 lemon
- ¼ cup lemon juice, freshly squeezed
- Salt and pepper to taste

Directions:

1. Place all ingredients in a Ziploc bag and allow to marinate for at least 6 hours in the fridge.
2. Preheat the oven to 350F.
3. Place the chicken–sauce and all–into a skillet.
4. Put the skillet in the oven and bake for 1 hour or until the chicken is tender.

Nutrition Info:

- Info Per Servings 6.2g Carbs, 48.2g Protein, 42.4g Fat, 610 Calories

Baked Pecorino Toscano Chicken

Servings: 4
Cooking Time: 60 Minutes
Ingredients:

- 4 chicken breasts, skinless and boneless
- ½ cup mayonnaise
- ½ cup buttermilk
- Salt and ground black pepper, to taste
- ¾ cup Pecorino Toscano cheese, grated
- Cooking spray
- 8 mozzarella cheese slices
- 1 tsp garlic powder

Directions:

1. Spray a baking dish, add in the chicken breasts, and top 2 mozzarella cheese slices to each piece. Using a bowl, combine the Pecorino cheese, pepper, buttermilk, mayonnaise, salt, and garlic. Sprinkle this over the chicken, set the dish in the oven at 370ºF, and bake for 1 hour.

Nutrition Info:

- Info Per Servings 6g Carbs, 20g Protein, 24g Fat, 346 Calories

Fish And Seafood Recipes

Buttery Almond Lemon Tilapia

Servings: 4

Cooking Time: 10 Minutes

Ingredients:

- 4 tilapia fillets
- 1/4 cup butter, cubed
- 1/4 cup white wine or chicken broth
- 2 tablespoons lemon juice
- 1/4 cup sliced almonds
- 1/2 teaspoon salt
- 1/4 teaspoon pepper
- 1 tablespoon olive oil

Directions:

1. Sprinkle fillets with salt and pepper. In a large nonstick skillet, heat oil over medium heat.
2. Add fillets; cook until fish just begins to flake easily with a fork, 2-3 minutes on each side. Remove and keep warm.
3. Add butter, wine and lemon juice to the same pan; cook and stir until butter is melted.
4. Serve with fish; sprinkle with almonds.

Nutrition Info:

- Info Per Servings 2g Carbs, 22g Protein, 19g Fat, 269 Calories

Coconut Curry Mussels

Servings: 6

Cooking Time: 25 Minutes

Ingredients:

- 3 lb mussels, cleaned, de-bearded
- 1 cup minced shallots
- 3 tbsp minced garlic
- 1 ½ cups coconut milk
- 2 cups dry white wine
- 2 tsp red curry powder
- ⅓ cup coconut oil
- ⅓ cup chopped green onions
- ⅓ cup chopped parsley

Directions:

1. Pour the wine into a large saucepan and cook the shallots and garlic over low heat. Stir in the coconut milk and red curry powder and cook for 3 minutes.
2. Add the mussels and steam for 7 minutes or until their shells are opened. Then, use a slotted spoon to remove to a bowl leaving the sauce in the pan. Discard any closed mussels at this point.
3. Stir the coconut oil into the sauce, turn the heat off, and stir in the parsley and green onions. Serve the sauce immediately with a butternut squash mash.

Nutrition Info:

- Info Per Servings 0.3g Carbs, 21.1g Protein, 20.6g Fat, 356 Calories

Cod In Garlic Butter Sauce

Servings: 6
Cooking Time: 20 Minutes
Ingredients:

- 2 tsp olive oil
- 6 Alaska cod fillets
- Salt and black pepper to taste
- 4 tbsp salted butter
- 4 cloves garlic, minced
- ⅓ cup lemon juice
- 3 tbsp white wine
- 2 tbsp chopped chives

Directions:

1. Heat the oil in a skillet over medium heat and season the cod with salt and black pepper. Fry the fillets in the oil for 4 minutes on one side, flip and cook for 1 minute. Take out, plate, and set aside.

2. In another skillet over low heat, melt the butter and sauté the garlic for 3 minutes. Add the lemon juice, wine, and chives. Season with salt, black pepper, and cook for 3 minutes until the wine slightly reduces. Put the fish in the skillet, spoon sauce over, cook for 30 seconds and turn the heat off.

3. Divide fish into 6 plates, top with sauce, and serve with buttered green beans.

Nutrition Info:

- Info Per Servings 2.3g Carbs, 20g Protein, 17.3g Fat, 264 Calories

Tilapia With Olives & Tomato Sauce

Servings: 4
Cooking Time: 30 Minutes
Ingredients:

- 4 tilapia fillets
- 2 garlic cloves, minced
- 2 tsp oregano
- 14 ounces diced tomatoes
- 1 tbsp olive oil
- ½ red onion, chopped
- 2 tbsp parsley
- ¼ cup kalamata olives

Directions:

1. Heat the olive oil in a skillet over medium heat and cook the onion for about 3 minutes. Add garlic and oregano and cook for 30 seconds. Stir in tomatoes and bring the mixture to a boil. Reduce the heat and simmer for 5 minutes. Add olives and tilapia, and cook for about 8 minutes. Serve the tilapia with tomato sauce.

Nutrition Info:

- Info Per Servings 6g Carbs, 23g Protein, 15g Fat, 282 Calories

Golden Pompano In Microwave

Servings: 2

Cooking Time: 11 Minutes

Ingredients:

- ½-lb pompano
- 1 tbsp soy sauce, low sodium
- 1-inch thumb ginger, diced
- 1 lemon, halved
- 1 stalk green onions, chopped
- ¼ cup water
- 1 tsp pepper
- 4 tbsp olive oil

Directions:

1. In a microwavable casserole dish, mix well all ingredients except for pompano, green onions, and lemon.
2. Squeeze half of the lemon in dish and slice into thin circles the other half.
3. Place pompano in the dish and add lemon circles on top of the fish. Drizzle with pepper and olive oil.
4. Cover top of a casserole dish with a microwave-safe plate.
5. Microwave for 5 minutes.
6. Remove from microwave, turn over fish, sprinkle green onions, top with a microwavable plate.
7. Return to microwave and cook for another 3 minutes.
8. Let it rest for 3 minutes more.
9. Serve and enjoy.

Nutrition Info:

- Info Per Servings 6.3g Carbs, 22.2g Protein, 39.5g Fat, 464 Calories

Coconut Crab Patties

Servings: 8

Cooking Time: 15 Minutes

Ingredients:

- 2 tbsp coconut oil
- 1 tbsp lemon juice
- 1 cup lump crab meat
- 2 tsp Dijon mustard
- 1 egg, beaten
- 1 ½ tbsp coconut flour

Directions:

1. In a bowl to the crabmeat add all the ingredients, except for the oil; mix well to combine. Make patties out of the mixture. Melt the coconut oil in a skillet over medium heat. Add the crab patties and cook for about 2-3 minutes per side.

Nutrition Info:

- Info Per Servings 3.6g Carbs, 15.3g Protein, 11.5g Fat, 215 Calories

Flounder With Dill And Capers

Servings: 4

Cooking Time: 15 Minutes

Ingredients:

- 4 flounder fillets
- 1 tbsp. chopped fresh dill
- 2 tbsp. capers, chopped
- 4 lemon wedges
- 6 tbsp olive oil
- Salt and pepper to taste

Directions:

1. Place a trivet in a large saucepan and pour a cup or two of water into the pan. Bring to a boil.
2. Place flounder in a heatproof dish that fits inside a saucepan. Season snapper with pepper and salt. Drizzle with olive oil on all sides. Sprinkle dill and capers on top of the filet.
3. Seal dish with foil. Place the dish on the trivet inside the saucepan. Cover and steam for 15 minutes.
4. Serve and enjoy with lemon wedges.

Nutrition Info:

- Info Per Servings 8.6g Carbs, 20.3g Protein, 35.9g Fat, 447 Calories

Baked Codfish With Lemon

Serves: 4
Cooking Time:25 Minutes
Ingredients:

- 4 fillets codfish
- 1 teaspoon salt
- 1 teaspoon pepper
- 2 tablespoons olive oil
- 2 teaspoons dried basil
- 2 tablespoons melted butter
- 1 teaspoon dried thyme
- 1/3 teaspoon onion powder
- 2 lemons, juiced
- lemon wedges, for garnish

Directions:

1. Preheat the oven to 400°F.
2. In a medium bowl combine the lemon juice, onion powder, olive oil, dried basil and thyme. Stir well. Season the fillets with salt and pepper.
3. Top each fillet into the mixture. Then place the fillets into a medium baking dish, greased with melted butter.
4. Bake the codfish fillets for 15-20 minutes. Serve with fresh lemon wedges. Enjoy!

Nutrition Info:

- Per serving: 3.9g Carbs; 21.2g Protein; 23.6g Fat; 308 Calories

Coconut Milk Sauce Over Crabs

Servings: 6
Cooking Time: 20 Minutes
Ingredients:

- 2-pounds crab quartered
- 1 can coconut milk
- 1 thumb-size ginger, sliced
- 1 onion, chopped
- 3 cloves of garlic, minced
- Pepper and salt to taste

Directions:

1. Place a heavy-bottomed pot on medium-high fire and add all ingredients.
2. Cover and bring to a boil, lower fire to a simmer, and simmer for 20 minutes.
3. Serve and enjoy.

Nutrition Info:

- Info Per Servings 6.3g Carbs, 29.3g Protein, 11.3g Fat, 244.1 Calories

Baked Calamari And Shrimp

Serves: 1

Cooking Time: 20 Minutes

Ingredients:

- 8 ounces calamari, cut in medium rings
- 7 ounces shrimp, peeled and deveined
- 1 eggs
- 3 tablespoons coconut flour
- 1 tablespoon coconut oil
- 2 tablespoons avocado, chopped
- 1 teaspoon tomato paste
- 1 tablespoon mayonnaise
- A splash of Worcestershire sauce
- 1 teaspoon lemon juice
- 2 lemon slices
- Salt and black pepper to the taste
- ½ teaspoon turmeric

Directions:

1. In a bowl, whisk egg with coconut oil.
2. Add calamari rings and shrimp and toss to coat.
3. In another bowl, mix flour with salt, pepper and turmeric and stir.
4. Dredge calamari and shrimp in this mix, place everything on a lined baking sheet, introduce in the oven at 400 °F and bake for 10 minutes.
5. Flip calamari and shrimp and bake for 10 minutes more.
6. Meanwhile, in a bowl, mix avocado with mayo and tomato paste and mash using a fork.
7. Add Worcestershire sauce, lemon juice, salt and pepper and stir well.
8. Divide baked calamari and shrimp on plates and serve with the sauce and lemon juice on the side.
9. Enjoy!

Nutrition Info:

- 10 carbs; 34 protein; 23 fat; 368 calories

Mustard-crusted Salmon

Servings: 4

Cooking Time: 15 Minutes

Ingredients:

- 1 ¼ lb. salmon fillets, cut into 4 portions
- 2 tsp. lemon juice
- 2 tbsp. stone-ground mustard
- Lemon wedges, for garnish
- 4 tbsp olive oil
- Salt and pepper to taste

Directions:

1. Place a trivet in a large saucepan and pour a cup of water into the pan. Bring to a boil.
2. Place salmon in a heatproof dish that fits inside saucepan and drizzle with olive oil. Season the salmon fillets with salt, pepper, and lemon juice. Sprinkle with mustard on top and garnish with lemon wedges on top. Seal dish with foil.
3. Place the dish on the trivet inside the saucepan. Cover and steam for 15 minutes.
4. Serve and enjoy.

Nutrition Info:

- Info Per Servings 2.9g Carbs, 29g Protein, 24.8g Fat, 360 Calories

Blackened Fish Tacos With Slaw

Servings: 4
Cooking Time: 20 Minutes

Ingredients:

- 1 tbsp olive oil
- 1 tsp chili powder
- 2 tilapia fillets
- 1 tsp paprika
- 4 low carb tortillas
- Slaw:
- ½ cup red cabbage, shredded
- 1 tbsp lemon juice
- 1 tsp apple cider vinegar
- 1 tbsp olive oil

Directions:

1. Season the tilapia with chili powder and paprika. Heat the olive oil in a skillet over medium heat.
2. Add tilapia and cook until blackened, about 3 minutes per side. Cut into strips. Divide the tilapia between the tortillas. Combine all slaw ingredients in a bowl. Split the slaw among the tortillas.

Nutrition Info:

- Info Per Servings 3.5g Carbs, 13.8g Protein, 20g Fat, 268 Calories

Lemon-rosemary Shrimps

Servings: 4
Cooking Time: 12 Minutes

Ingredients:

- ½ cup lemon juice, freshly squeezed
- 1 ½ lb. shrimps, peeled and deveined
- 2 tbsp fresh rosemary
- ¼ cup coconut aminos
- 2 tbsp butter
- Pepper to taste
- 4 tbsp olive oil

Directions:

1. Place a nonstick saucepan on medium-high fire and heat oil and butter for 2 minutes.
2. Stir in shrimps and coconut aminos. Season with pepper. Sauté for 5 minutes.
3. Add remaining ingredients and cook for another 5 minutes while stirring frequently.
4. Serve and enjoy.

Nutrition Info:

- Info Per Servings 3.7g Carbs, 35.8g Protein, 22.4g Fat, 359 Calories

Boiled Garlic Clams

Servings: 6
Cooking Time: 10 Minutes

Ingredients:

- 3 tbsp butter
- 6 cloves of garlic
- 50 small clams in the shell, scrubbed
- ½ cup fresh parsley, chopped
- 4 tbsp. extra virgin olive oil
- 1 cup water
- Salt and pepper to taste

Directions:

1. Heat the olive oil and butter in a large pot placed on medium-high fire for a minute.
2. Stir in the garlic and cook until fragrant and slightly browned.
3. Stir in the clams, water, and parsley. Season with salt and pepper to taste.
4. Cover and cook for 5 minutes or until clams have opened.
5. Discard unopened clams and serve.

Nutrition Info:

- Info Per Servings 0.9g Carbs, 11.3g Protein, 12.8g Fat, 159 Calories

Seared Scallops With Chorizo And Asiago Cheese

Servings: 4

Cooking Time: 15 Minutes

Ingredients:

- 2 tbsp ghee
- 16 fresh scallops
- 8 ounces chorizo, chopped
- 1 red bell pepper, seeds removed, sliced
- 1 cup red onions, finely chopped
- 1 cup asiago cheese, grated
- Salt and black pepper to taste

Directions:

1. Melt half of the ghee in a skillet over medium heat, and cook the onion and bell pepper for 5 minutes until tender. Add the chorizo and stir-fry for another 3 minutes. Remove and set aside.
2. Pat dry the scallops with paper towels, and season with salt and pepper. Add the remaining ghee to the skillet and sear the scallops for 2 minutes on each side to have a golden brown color. Add the chorizo mixture back and warm through. Transfer to serving platter and top with asiago cheese.

Nutrition Info:

- Info Per Servings 5g Carbs, 36g Protein, 32g Fat, 491 Calories

Shrimp And Cauliflower Jambalaya

Servings: 4

Cooking Time: 15 Minutes

Ingredients:

- 2 cloves garlic, peeled and minced
- 1 head cauliflower, grated
- 1 cup chopped tomatoes
- 8 oz. raw shrimp, peeled and deveined
- 1 tbsp Cajun seasoning
- Salt and pepper
- 4 tbsp coconut oil
- 1 tbsp water

Directions:

1. On medium-high fire, heat a nonstick saucepan for 2 minutes. Add oil to a pan and swirl to coat bottom and sides. Heat oil for a minute.
2. Add garlic and sauté for a minute. Stir in tomatoes and stir fry for 5 minutes. Add water and deglaze the pan.
3. Add remaining ingredients. Season generously with pepper.
4. Increase fire to high and stir fry for 3 minutes.
5. Lower fire to low, cover, and cook for 5 minutes.
6. Serve and enjoy.

Nutrition Info:

- Info Per Servings 7.8g Carbs, 21.4g Protein, 22.25g Fat, 314 Calories

Sautéed Savory Shrimps

Servings: 8

Cooking Time: 15 Minutes

Ingredients:

- 2 pounds shrimp, peeled and deveined
- 4 cloves garlic, minced
- ½ cup chicken stock, low sodium
- 1 tablespoon lemon juice
- Salt and pepper
- 5 tablespoons oil

Directions:

1. Place a heavy-bottomed pot on medium-high fire and heat pot for 3 minutes.
2. Once hot, add oil and stir around to coat pot with oil.
3. Sauté the garlic and corn for 5 minutes.
4. Add remaining ingredients and mix well.
5. Cover and bring to a boil, lower fire to a simmer, and simmer for 5 minutes.
6. Serve and enjoy.

Nutrition Info:

- Info Per Servings 1.7g Carbs, 25.2g Protein, 9.8g Fat, 182.6 Calories

Seasoned Salmon With Parmesan

Servings: 4

Cooking Time: 20 Mins

Ingredients:

- 2 lbs. salmon fillet
- 3 minced garlic cloves
- ¼ cup. chopped parsley
- ½ cup. grated parmesan cheese
- Salt and pepper to taste

Directions:

1. Preheat oven to 425 degrees F. Line a baking sheet with parchment paper.
2. Lay salmon fillets on the lined baking sheet, season with salt and pepper to taste.
3. Bake for 10 minutes. Remove from the oven and sprinkle with garlic, parmesan and parsley.
4. Place in the oven to cook for 5 more minutes. Transfer to plates before serving.

Nutrition Info:

- Info Per Servings 0.6g Carbs, 25g Protein, 12g Fat, 210 Calories

Angel Hair Shirataki With Creamy Shrimp

Serves:4

Cooking Time: 25 Minutes

Ingredients:

- 2 (8 oz) packs angel hair shirataki noodles
- 1 tbsp olive oil
- 1 lb shrimp, deveined
- 2 tbsp unsalted butter
- 6 garlic cloves, minced
- ½ cup dry white wine
- 1 ½ cups heavy cream
- ½ cup grated Asiago cheese
- 2 tbsp chopped fresh parsley

Directions:

1. Heat olive oil in a skillet, season the shrimp with salt and pepper, and cook on both sides, 2 minutes; set aside. Melt butter in the skillet and sauté garlic. Stir in wine and cook until reduced by half, scraping the bottom of the pan to deglaze. Stir in heavy cream. Let simmer for 1 minute and stir in Asiago cheese to melt. Return the shrimp to the sauce and sprinkle the parsley on top. Bring 2 cups of water to a boi. Strain shirataki pasta and rinse under hot running water. Allow proper draining and pour the shirataki pasta into the boiling water. Cook for 3 minutes and strain again. Place a dry skillet and stir-fry the pasta until dry, 1-2 minutes. Season with salt and plate. Top with the shrimp sauce and serve.

Nutrition Info:

- Per Serves 6.3g Carbs; 33g Protein ; 32g Fats; 493 Calories

Cilantro Shrimp

Servings: 4
Cooking Time: 10 Minutes
Ingredients:

* 1/2 cup reduced-fat Asian sesame salad dressing
* 1-pound uncooked shrimp, peeled and deveined
* Lime wedges
* 1/4 cup chopped fresh cilantro
* 5 tablespoon olive oil
* Salt and pepper

Directions:

1. In a large nonstick skillet, heat 1 tablespoon dressing over medium heat. Add shrimp; cook and stir 1 minute.
2. Stir in remaining dressing; cook, uncovered, until shrimp turn pink, 1-2 minutes longer.
3. To serve, squeeze lime juice over the top; sprinkle with cilantro, pepper, and salt. If desired, serve with rice.

Nutrition Info:

* Info Per Servings 4.7g Carbs, 32g Protein, 39g Fat, 509 Calories

Baked Fish With Feta And Tomato

Serves: 2
Cooking Time: 15 Minutes
Ingredients:

* 2 pacific whitening fillets
* 1 scallion, chopped
* 1 Roma tomato, chopped
* 1 tsp fresh oregano
* 1-ounce feta cheese, crumbled
* Seasoning:
* 2 tbsp avocado oil
* 1/3 tsp salt
* 1/4 tsp ground black pepper
* ¼ crushed red pepper

Directions:

1. Turn on the oven, then set it to 400 °F and let it preheat.Take a medium skillet pan, place it over medium heat, add oil and when hot, add scallion and cook for 3 minutes.Add tomatoes, stir in ½ tsp oregano, 1/8 tsp salt, black pepper, red pepper, pour in ¼ cup water and bring it to simmer.Sprinkle remaining salt over fillets, add to the pan, drizzle with remaining oil, and then bake for 10 to 12 minutes until fillets are fork-tender.When done, top fish with remaining oregano and cheese and then serve.

Nutrition Info:

* 8 g Carbs; 26.7 g Protein; 29.5 g Fats; 427.5 Calories

Halibut With Pesto

Servings: 4
Cooking Time: 15 Minutes
Ingredients:

- 4 halibut fillets
- 1 cup basil leaves
- 2 cloves of garlic, minced
- 1 tbsp. lemon juice, freshly squeezed
- 2 tbsp pine nuts
- 2 tbsp. oil, preferably extra virgin olive oil
- Salt and pepper to taste

Directions:

1. In a food processor, pulse the basil, olive oil, pine nuts, garlic, and lemon juice until coarse. Season with salt and pepper to taste.
2. Place a trivet in a large saucepan and pour a cup or two of water into the pan. Bring to a boil.
3. Place salmon in a heatproof dish that fits inside a saucepan. Season salmon with pepper and salt. Drizzle with pesto sauce.
4. Seal dish with foil. Place the dish on the trivet inside the saucepan. Cover and steam for 15 minutes.
5. Serve and enjoy.

Nutrition Info:

- Info Per Servings 0.8g Carbs, 75.8g Protein, 8.4g Fat, 401 Calories

Lemon Marinated Salmon With Spices

Servings: 2
Cooking Time: 15 Minutes
Ingredients:

- 2 tablespoons. lemon juice
- 1 tablespoon. yellow miso paste
- 2 teaspoons. Dijon mustard
- 1 pinch cayenne pepper and sea salt to taste
- 2 center-cut salmon fillets, boned; skin on
- 1 1/2 tablespoons mayonnaise
- 1 tablespoon ground black pepper

Directions:

1. In a bowl, combine lemon juice with black pepper. Stir in mayonnaise, miso paste, Dijon mustard, and cayenne pepper, mix well. Pour over salmon fillets, reserve about a tablespoon marinade. Cover and marinate the fish in the refrigerator for 30 minutes.
2. Preheat oven to 450 degrees F. Line a baking sheet with parchment paper.
3. Lay fillets on the prepared baking sheet. Rub the reserved lemon-pepper marinade on fillets. Then season with cayenne pepper and sea salt to taste.
4. Bake in the oven for 10 to 15 minutes until cooked through.

Nutrition Info:

- Info Per Servings 7.1g Carbs, 20g Protein, 28.1g Fat, 361 Calories

Enchilada Sauce On Mahi Mahi

Servings: 2
Cooking Time: 15 Minutes
Ingredients:

- 2 Mahi fillets, fresh
- ¼ cup commercial enchilada sauce
- Pepper to taste

Directions:

1. In a heat-proof dish that fits inside saucepan, place fish and top with enchilada sauce.
2. Place a large saucepan on the medium-high fire. Place a trivet inside the saucepan and fill the pan halfway with water. Cover and bring to a boil.
3. Cover dish with foil and place on a trivet.
4. Cover pan and steam for 10 minutes. Let it rest in pan for another 5 minutes.
5. Serve and enjoy topped with pepper.

Nutrition Info:

- Info Per Servings 8.9g Carbs, 19.8g Protein, 15.9g Fat, 257 Calories

Salmon And Cauliflower Rice Pilaf

Servings: 4

Cooking Time: 25 Minutes

Ingredients:

- 1 cauliflower head, shredded
- ¼ cup dried vegetable soup mix
- 1 cup chicken broth
- 1 pinch saffron
- 1-lb wild salmon fillets
- 6 tbsp olive oil
- Pepper and salt to taste

Directions:

1. Place a heavy-bottomed pot on medium-high fire and add all ingredients and mix well.
2. Bring to a boil, lower fire to a simmer, and simmer for 10 minutes.
3. Turn off fire, shred salmon, adjust seasoning to taste.
4. Let it rest for 5 minutes.
5. Fluff again, serve, and enjoy.

Nutrition Info:

- Info Per Servings 4.7g Carbs, 31.8g Protein, 31.5g Fat, 429 Calories

Grilled Shrimp With Chimichurri Sauce

Servings: 4

Cooking Time: 55 Minutes

Ingredients:

- 1 pound shrimp, peeled and deveined
- 2 tbsp olive oil
- Juice of 1 lime
- Chimichurri
- ½ tsp salt
- ¼ cup olive oil
- 2 garlic cloves
- ¼ cup red onion, chopped
- ¼ cup red wine vinegar
- ½ tsp pepper
- 2 cups parsley
- ¼ tsp red pepper flakes

Directions:

1. Process the chimichurri ingredients in a blender until smooth; set aside. Combine shrimp, olive oil, and lime juice, in a bowl, and let marinate in the fridge for 30 minutes. Preheat your grill to medium. Add shrimp and cook about 2 minutes per side. Serve shrimp drizzled with the chimichurri sauce.

Nutrition Info:

- Info Per Servings 3.5g Carbs, 16g Protein, 20.3g Fat, 283 Calories

Vegan, Vegetable & Meatless Recipes

Grilled Cauliflower

Servings: 8
Cooking Time: 20 Minutes
Ingredients:

- 1 large head cauliflower
- 1 teaspoon ground turmeric
- 1/2 teaspoon crushed red pepper flakes
- Lemon juice, additional olive oil, and pomegranate seeds, optional
- 2 tablespoons olive oil
- 2 tablespoons melted butter

Directions:

1. Remove leaves and trim stem from cauliflower. Cut cauliflower into eight wedges. Mix turmeric and pepper flakes. Brush wedges with oil; sprinkle with turmeric mixture.
2. Grill, covered, over medium-high heat or broil 4 minutes from heat until cauliflower is tender, 8-10 minutes on each side. If desired, drizzle with lemon juice and additional oil. Brush with melted butter and serve with pomegranate seeds.

Nutrition Info:

- Info Per Servings 2.3g Carbs, 0.7g Protein, 6.3g Fat, 66 Calories

Cauliflower Mac And Cheese

Servings: 7
Cooking Time: 45 Minutes
Ingredients:

- 1 cauliflower head, riced
- 1 ½ cups shredded cheese
- 2 tsp paprika
- ¾ tsp rosemary
- 2 tsp turmeric
- 3 eggs
- Olive oil, for frying

Directions:

1. Microwave the cauliflower for 5 minutes. Place it in cheesecloth and squeeze the extra juices out. Place the cauliflower in a bowl. Stir in the rest of the ingredients.
2. Heat the oil in a deep pan until it reaches 360ºF. Add the 'mac and cheese' and fry until golden and crispy. Drain on paper towels before serving.

Nutrition Info:

- Info Per Servings 2g Carbs, 8.6g Protein, 12g Fat, 160 Calories

Creamy Almond And Turnip Soup

Servings: 4
Cooking Time: 25 Minutes
Ingredients:
- 1 tbsp olive oil
- 1 cup onion, chopped
- 1 celery, chopped
- 2 cloves garlic, minced
- 2 turnips, peeled and chopped
- 4 cups vegetable broth
- Salt and white pepper, to taste
- ¼ cup ground almonds
- 1 cup almond milk
- 1 tbsp fresh cilantro, chopped

Directions:
1. Set a stockpot over medium-high heat and warm the oil. Add in celery, garlic, and onion and sauté for 6 minutes. Stir in white pepper, broth, salt, and ground almonds. Boil the mixture. Set heat to low and simmer for 17 minutes. Transfer the soup to an immersion blender and puree. Decorate with fresh cilantro before serving.

Nutrition Info:
- Info Per Servings 9.2g Carbs, 3.8g Protein, 6.5g Fat, 114 Calories

Spaghetti Squash With Eggplant & Parmesan

Servings: 4
Cooking Time: 15 Minutes
Ingredients:
- 1 tbsp butter
- 1 cup cherry tomatoes
- 2 tbsp parsley
- 1 eggplant, cubed
- ¼ cup Parmesan cheese
- 3 tbsp scallions, chopped
- 1 cup snap peas
- 1 tsp lemon zest
- 2 cups cooked spaghetti squash

Directions:
1. Melt the butter in a saucepan and cook eggplant for 5 minutes until tender. Add the tomatoes and peas, and cook for 5 more minutes. Stir in parsley, zest, and scallions, and remove the pan from heat. Stir in spaghetti squash and parmesan.

Nutrition Info:
- Info Per Servings 6.8g Carbs, 6.9g Protein, 8.2g Fat, 139 Calories

Zucchini Boats

Servings: 4
Cooking Time: 50 Minutes
Ingredients:

- 1 tbsp olive oil
- 12 ounces firm tofu, drained and crumbled
- 2 garlic cloves, pressed
- ½ cup onions, chopped
- 2 cups tomato paste
- ¼ tsp turmeric
- Sea salt and chili pepper, to taste
- 3 zucchinis, cut into halves, scoop out the insides
- 1 tbsp nutritional yeast
- ¼ cup almonds, chopped

Directions:

1. Set a pan over medium-high heat and warm oil; add in onion, garlic, and tofu and cook for 5 minutes.Place in scooped zucchini flesh, all seasonings and 1 cup of tomato paste; cook for 6 more minutes, until the tofu starts to brown.
2. Set oven to 360ºF. Grease a baking dish with a cooking spray. Plate the tofu mixture among the zucchini shells. Arrange the stuffed zucchini shells in the baking dish. Stir in the remaining 1 cup of tomato paste. Bake for about 30 minutes. Sprinkle with almonds and Nutritional yeast and continue baking for 5 to 6 more minutes.

Nutrition Info:

- Info Per Servings 9.8g Carbs, 7.5g Protein, 10g Fat, 148 Calories

Egg And Tomato Salad

Servings: 2
Cooking Time: 1 Minute
Ingredients:

- 4 hard-boiled eggs, peeled and sliced
- 2 red tomatoes, chopped
- 1 small red onion, chopped
- 2 tablespoons lemon juice, freshly squeezed
- Salt and pepper to taste
- 4 tablespoons olive oil

Directions:

1. Place all ingredients in a mixing bowl.
2. Toss to coat all ingredients.
3. Garnish with parsley if desired.
4. Serve over toasted whole wheat bread.

Nutrition Info:

- Info Per Servings 9.1g Carbs, 14.7g Protein, 15.9g Fat, 189 Calories

Keto Cauliflower Hash Browns

Servings: 4

Cooking Time: 30 Mins

Ingredients:

- 1 lb cauliflower
- 3 eggs
- ½ yellow onion, grated
- 2 pinches pepper
- 4 oz. butter, for frying
- What you'll need from the store cupboard:
- 1 tsp salt

Directions:

1. Rinse, trim and grate the cauliflower using a food processor or grater.

2. In a large bowl, add the cauliflower onion and pepper, tossing evenly. Set aside for 5 to 10 minutes.

3. In a large skillet over medium heat, heat a generous amount of butter on medium heat. The cooking process will go quicker if you plan to have room for 3–4 pancakes at a time. Use the oven on low heat to keep the first batches of pancakes warm while you make the others.

4. Place scoops of the grated cauliflower mixture in the frying pan and flatten them carefully until they measure about 3 to 4 inches in diameter.

5. Fry for 4 to 5 minutes on each side. Adjust the heat to make sure they don't burn. Serve.

Nutrition Info:

- Info Per Servings 5g Carbs, 7g Protein, 26g Fat, 282 Calories

Roasted Brussels Sprouts With Sunflower Seeds

Servings: 6

Cooking Time: 45 Minutes

Ingredients:

- Nonstick cooking spray
- 3 pounds brussels sprouts, halved
- ¼ cup olive oil
- Salt and ground black pepper, to taste
- 1 tsp sunflower seeds
- 2 tbsp fresh chives, chopped

Directions:

1. Set oven to 390ºF. Apply a nonstick cooking spray to a rimmed baking sheet. Arrange sprout halves on the baking sheet. Shake in black pepper, salt, sunflower seeds, and olive oil.

2. Roast for 40 minutes, until the cabbage becomes soft. Apply a garnish of fresh chopped chives.

Nutrition Info:

- Info Per Servings 8g Carbs, 2.1g Protein, 17g Fat, 186 Calories

Roasted Asparagus With Spicy Eggplant Dip

Servings: 6

Cooking Time: 35 Minutes

Ingredients:

- 1 ½ pounds asparagus spears, trimmed
- ¼ cup olive oil
- 1 tsp sea salt
- ½ tsp black pepper, to taste
- ½ tsp paprika
- For Eggplant Dip
- ¾ pound eggplants
- 2 tsp olive oil
- ½ cup scallions, chopped
- 2 cloves garlic, minced
- 1 tbsp fresh lemon juice
- ½ tsp chili pepper
- Salt and black pepper, to taste
- ¼ cup fresh cilantro, chopped

Directions:

1. Set the oven to 390ºF. Line a parchment paper to a baking sheet. Add asparagus spears to the baking sheet. Toss with oil, paprika, pepper, and salt. Bake until cooked through for 9 minutes.
2. Set the oven to 425 ºF. Add eggplants on a lined cookie sheet. Place under the broiler for about 20 minutes; let the eggplants to cool. Peel them and discard the stems. Place a frying pan over medium-high heat and warm olive oil. Add in garlic and onion and sauté until tender.
3. Using a food processor, pulse together black pepper, roasted eggplants, salt, lemon juice, scallion mixture, and chili pepper to mix evenly. Add cilantro for garnishing. Serve alongside roasted asparagus spears.

Nutrition Info:

- Info Per Servings 9g Carbs, 3.6g Protein, 12.1g Fat, 149 Calories

Grated Cauliflower With Seasoned Mayo

Servings: 2

Cooking Time: 15 Mins

Ingredients:

- 1 lb grated cauliflower
- 3 oz. butter
- 4 eggs
- 3 oz. pimientos de padron or poblano peppers
- ½ cup mayonnaise
- 1 tsp olive oil
- Salt and pepper
- 1 tsp garlic powder (optional)

Directions:

1. In a bowl, whisk together the mayonnaise and garlic and set aside.
2. Rinse, trim and grate the cauliflower using a food processor or grater.
3. Melt a generous amount of butter and fry grated cauliflower for about 5 minutes. Season salt and pepper to taste.
4. Fry poblanos with oil until lightly crispy. Then fry eggs as you want and sprinkle salt and pepper over them.
5. Serve with poblanos and cauliflower. Drizzle some mayo mixture on top.

Nutrition Info:

- Info Per Servings 9g Carbs, 17g Protein, 87g Fat, 898 Calories

Creamy Artichoke And Spinach

Servings: 4
Cooking Time: 15 Minutes
Ingredients:

* 5 tablespoons olive oil
* 1 can water-packed artichoke hearts quartered
* 1 package frozen spinach
* 1 cup shredded part-skim mozzarella cheese, divided
* 1/4 cup grated Parmesan cheese
* 1/2 teaspoon salt
* 1/4 teaspoon pepper

Directions:

1. Heat oil in a pan over medium flame. Add artichoke hearts and season with salt and pepper to taste. Cook for 5 minutes. Stir in the spinach until wilted.
2. Place in a bowl and stir in mozzarella cheese, Parmesan cheese, salt, and pepper. Toss to combine.
3. Transfer to a greased 2-qt. Broiler-safe baking dish; sprinkle with remaining mozzarella cheese. Broil 4-6 in. from heat 2-3 minutes or until cheese is melted.

Nutrition Info:

* Info Per Servings 7.3g Carbs, 11.5g Protein, 23.9g Fat, 283 Calories

Zoodles With Avocado & Olives

Servings: 4
Cooking Time: 15 Minutes
Ingredients:

* 4 zucchinis, julienned or spiralized
* ¼ cup chopped basil
* ½ cup pesto
* 2 tbsp olive oil
* 2 avocados, sliced
* ¼ cup chopped sun-dried tomatoes
* 1 cup kalamata olives, chopped

Directions:

1. Heat half of the olive oil in a pan over medium heat. Add zoodles and cook for 4 minutes. Transfer to a plate. Stir in pesto, basil, salt, tomatoes, and olives. Top with avocado slices.

Nutrition Info:

* Info Per Servings 8.4g Carbs, 6.3g Protein, 42g Fat, 449 Calories

Creamy Kale And Mushrooms

Servings: 3
Cooking Time: 15 Minutes
Ingredients:

* 3 cloves of garlic, minced
* 1 cup heavy cream
* 1 onion, chopped
* 5 tablespoons oil
* 1 bunch kale, stems removed and leaves chopped
* Salt and pepper to taste
* 3 white button mushrooms, chopped

Directions:

1. Heat oil in a pot.
2. Sauté the garlic and onion until fragrant for 2 minutes.
3. Stir in mushrooms. Season with pepper and salt. Cook for 8 minutes.
4. Stir in kale and coconut milk. Simmer for 5 minutes.
5. Adjust seasoning to taste.

Nutrition Info:

* Info Per Servings 7.9g Carbs, 6.0g Protein, 35.5g Fat, 365 Calories

Endives Mix With Lemon Dressing

Servings: 8

Cooking Time: 0 Minutes

Ingredients:

- 1 bunch watercress
- 2 heads endive, halved lengthwise and thinly sliced
- 1 cup pomegranate seeds
- 1 shallot, thinly sliced
- 2 lemons, juiced and zested
- 1/4 teaspoon salt
- 1/8 teaspoon pepper
- 1/4 cup olive oil

Directions:

1. In a large bowl, combine watercress, endive, pomegranate seeds, and shallot.
2. In a small bowl, whisk the lemon juice, zest, salt, pepper, and olive oil. Drizzle over salad; toss to coat.

Nutrition Info:

- Info Per Servings 6g Carbs, 2g Protein, 13g Fat, 151 Calories

Colorful Vegan Soup

Servings: 6

Cooking Time: 25 Minutes

Ingredients:

- 2 tsp olive oil
- 1 red onion, chopped
- 2 cloves garlic, minced
- 1 celery stalk, chopped
- 1 head broccoli, chopped
- 1 carrot, sliced
- 1 cup spinach, torn into pieces
- 1 cup collard greens, chopped
- Sea salt and black pepper, to taste
- 2 thyme sprigs, chopped
- 1 rosemary sprig, chopped
- 2 bay leaves
- 6 cups vegetable stock
- 2 tomatoes, chopped
- 1 cup almond milk
- 1 tbsp white miso paste
- ½ cup arugula

Directions:

1. Place a large pot over medium-high heat and warm oil. Add in carrots, celery, onion, broccoli, garlic, and sauté until soft.
2. Place in spinach, salt, rosemary, tomatoes, bay leaves, ground black pepper, collard greens, thyme, and vegetable stock. On low heat, simmer the mixture for 15 minutes while the lid is slightly open.
3. Stir in white miso paste, watercress, and almond milk and cook for 5 more minutes.

Nutrition Info:

- Info Per Servings 9g Carbs, 2.9g Protein, 11.4g Fat, 142 Calories

Sausage Roll

Servings: 6
Cooking Time: 1 Hour And 15 Minutes
Ingredients:

- 6 vegan sausages (defrosted)
- 1 cup mushrooms
- 1 onion
- 2 fresh sage leaves
- 1 package tofu skin sheet
- Salt and pepper to taste
- 5 tablespoons olive oil

Directions:

1. Preheat the oven to 180°F/356°F assisted.
2. Defrost the vegan sausages.
3. Roughly chop the mushrooms and add them to a food processor. Process until mostly broken down. Peel and roughly chop the onions, then add them to the processor along with the defrosted vegan sausages, sage leaves, and a pinch of salt and pepper. Pour in the oil. Process until all the ingredients have mostly broken down, and only a few larger pieces remain.
4. Heat a frying pan on a medium heat. Once hot, transfer the mushroom mixture to the pan and fry for 20 minutes or until almost all of the moisture has evaporated, frequently stirring to prevent the mixture sticking to the pan.
5. Remove the mushroom mixture from the heat and transfer to a plate. Leave to cool completely. Tip: if it's cold outside, we leave the mushroom mixture outdoors, so it cools quicker.
6. Meanwhile, either line a large baking tray with baking paper or (if the pastry already comes wrapped in a sheet of baking paper) roll out the tofu skin onto the tray and cut it in half both lengthways and widthways to create 4 equal-sized pieces of tofu skin.
7. Spoon a quarter of the mushroom mixture along the length of each rectangle of tofu skin and shape the mixture into a log. Add one vegan sausage and roll into a log.
8. Seal the roll by securing the edged with a toothpick.
9. Brush the sausage rolls with olive oil and bake for 40-45 minutes until golden brown. Enjoy!

Nutrition Info:

- Info Per Servings 3g Carbs, 0.9g Protein, 11g Fat, 113 Calories

Greek-style Zucchini Pasta

Servings: 4
Cooking Time: 15 Minutes
Ingredients:

- ¼ cup sun-dried tomatoes
- 5 garlic cloves, minced
- 2 tbsp butter
- 1 cup spinach
- 2 large zucchinis, spiralized
- ¼ cup crumbled feta
- ¼ cup Parmesan cheese, shredded
- 10 kalamata olives, halved
- 2 tbsp olive oil
- 2 tbsp chopped parsley

Directions:

1. Heat the olive oil in a pan over medium heat. Add zoodles, butter, garlic, and spinach. Cook for about 5 minutes. Stir in the olives, tomatoes, and parsley. Cook for 2 more minutes. Add in the cheeses and serve.

Nutrition Info:

- Info Per Servings 6.5g Carbs, 6.5g Protein, 19.5g Fat, 231 Calories

Creamy Cucumber Avocado Soup

Servings: 4

Cooking Time: 15 Minutes

Ingredients:

- 4 large cucumbers, seeded, chopped
- 1 large avocado, peeled and pitted
- Salt and black pepper to taste
- 2 cups water
- 1 tbsp cilantro, chopped
- 3 tbsp olive oil
- 2 limes, juiced
- 2 tsp minced garlic
- 2 tomatoes, evenly chopped
- 1 chopped avocado for garnish

Directions:

1. Pour the cucumbers, avocado halves, salt, pepper, olive oil, lime juice, cilantro, water, and garlic in the food processor. Puree the ingredients for 2 minutes or until smooth.

2. Pour the mixture in a bowl and top with avocado and tomatoes. Serve chilled with zero-carb bread.

Nutrition Info:

- Info Per Servings 4.1g Carbs, 3.7g Protein, 7.4g Fat, 170 Calories

Zucchini Noodles

Servings: 6

Cooking Time: 15 Mins

Ingredients:

- 2 cloves garlic, minced
- 2 medium zucchini, cut into noodles with a spiralizer
- 12 zucchini blossoms, pistils removed; cut into strips
- 6 fresh basil leaves, cut into strips, or to taste
- 4 tablespoons olive oil
- Salt to taste

Directions:

1. In a large skillet over low heat, cook garlic in olive oil for 10 minutes until slightly browned. Add in zucchini and zucchini blossoms, stir well.

2. Toss in green beans and season with salt to taste; sprinkle with basil and serve.

Nutrition Info:

- Info Per Servings 13.5g Carbs, 5.7g Protein, 28.1g Fat, 348 Calories

Cream Of Zucchini And Avocado

Servings: 4

Cooking Time: 35 Minutes

Ingredients:

- 3 tsp vegetable oil
- 1 onion, chopped
- 1 carrot, sliced
- 1 turnip, sliced
- 3 cups zucchinis, chopped
- 1 avocado, peeled and diced
- ¼ tsp ground black pepper
- 4 vegetable broth
- 1 tomato, pureed

Directions:

1. In a pot, warm the oil and sauté onion until translucent, about 3 minutes. Add in turnip, zucchini, and carrot and cook for 7 minutes; add black pepper for seasoning.

2. Mix in pureed tomato, and broth; and boil. Change heat to low and allow the mixture to simmer for 20 minutes. Lift from the heat. In batches, add the soup and avocado to a blender. Blend until creamy and smooth.

Nutrition Info:

- Info Per Servings 11g Carbs, 2.2g Protein, 13.4g Fat, 165 Calories

Vegetable Tempura

Servings: 4

Cooking Time: 17 Minutes

Ingredients:

- ½ cup coconut flour + extra for dredging
- Salt and black pepper to taste
- 3 egg yolks
- 2 red bell peppers, cut into strips
- 1 squash, peeled and cut into strips
- 1 broccoli, cut into florets
- 1 cup Chilled water
- Olive oil for frying
- Lemon wedges to serve
- Sugar-free soy sauce to serve

Directions:

1. In a deep frying pan or wok, heat the olive oil over medium heat. Beat the eggs lightly with ½ cup of coconut flour and water. The mixture should be lumpy. Dredge the vegetables lightly in some flour, shake off the excess flour, dip it in the batter, and then into the hot oil.

2. Fry in batches for 1 minute each, not more, and remove with a perforated spoon onto a wire rack. Sprinkle with salt and pepper and serve with the lemon wedges and soy sauce.

Nutrition Info:

- Info Per Servings 0.9g Carbs, 3g Protein, 17g Fat, 218 Calories

Keto Enchilada Bake

Servings: 6

Cooking Time: 20 Minutes

Ingredients:

- 1 package House Foods Organic Extra Firm Tofu
- 1 cup roma tomatoes, chopped
- 1 cup shredded cheddar cheese
- 1 small avocado, pitted and sliced
- ½ cup sour cream
- 5 tablespoons olive oil
- Salt and pepper to taste

Directions:

1. Preheat oven to 350F.
2. Cut tofu into small cubes and sauté with oil and seasoning. Set aside and reserve the oil.
3. Place the tofu in the bottom of a casserole dish.
4. Mix the reserved oil and tomatoes and pour over the tofu.
5. Sprinkle with cheese on top.
6. Bake for 20 minutes.
7. Top with avocado and sour cream toppings.
8. Serve and enjoy.

Nutrition Info:

- Info Per Servings 6g Carbs, 38g Protein, 40g Fat, 568 Calories

Cilantro-lime Guacamole

Servings: 4

Cooking Time: 10 Minutes

Ingredients:

- 3 avocados, peeled, pitted, and mashed
- 1 lime, juiced
- 1/2 cup diced onion
- 3 tablespoons chopped fresh cilantro
- 2 Roma (plum) tomatoes, diced
- 1 teaspoon salt
- 1 teaspoon minced garlic
- 1 pinch ground cayenne pepper (optional)
- 1 teaspoon minced garlic

Directions:

1. In a mixing bowl, mash the avocados with a fork. Sprinkle with salt and lime juice.
2. Stir together diced onion, tomatoes, cilantro, pepper and garlic.
3. Serve immediately, or refrigerate until ready to serve.

Nutrition Info:

- Info Per Servings 8g Carbs, 19g Protein, 22.2g Fat, 362 Calories

Roasted Leeks And Asparagus

Servings: 12

Cooking Time: 25 Minutes

Ingredients:

- 3 pounds fresh asparagus, trimmed
- 2 medium leeks (white portion only), halved lengthwise
- 1-1/2 teaspoons dill weed
- 1/2 teaspoon crushed red pepper flakes
- 3 tablespoons melted butter
- 1/4 teaspoon pepper
- 1/2 teaspoon salt
- 4 ½ tablespoons olive oil

Directions:

1. Place asparagus and leeks on an ungreased 15x10x1-inch baking pan. Combine the remaining ingredients; pour over vegetables.
2. Bake at 400F for 20-25 minutes or until tender, stirring occasionally.

Nutrition Info:

- Info Per Servings 6g Carbs, 3g Protein, 8g Fat, 98 Calories

Greek Styled Veggie-rice

Servings: 3

Cooking Time: 20 Minutes

Ingredients:

- 3 tbsp chopped fresh mint
- 1 small tomato, chopped
- 1 head cauliflower, cut into large florets
- ¼ cup fresh lemon juice
- ½ yellow onion, minced
- pepper and salt to taste
- ¼ cup extra virgin olive oil

Directions:

1. In a bowl, mix lemon juice and onion and leave for 30 minutes. Then drain onion and reserve the juice and onion bits.
2. In a blender, shred cauliflower until the size of a grain of rice.
3. On medium fire, place a medium nonstick skillet and for 8-10 minutes cook cauliflower while covered.
4. Add grape tomatoes and cook for 3 minutes while stirring occasionally.
5. Add mint and onion bits. Cook for another three minutes.
6. Meanwhile, in a small bowl whisk pepper, salt, 3 tbsp reserved lemon juice, and olive oil until well blended.
7. Remove cooked cauliflower, transfer to a serving bowl, pour lemon juice mixture, and toss to mix.
8. Before serving, if needed season with pepper and salt to taste.

Nutrition Info:

- Info Per Servings 4.0g Carbs, 2.3g Protein, 9.5g Fat, 120 Calories

Cauliflower Fritters

Servings: 6

Cooking Time: 15 Minutes

Ingredients:

- 1 large cauliflower head, cut into florets
- 2 eggs, beaten
- ½ teaspoon turmeric
- 1 large onion, peeled and chopped
- ½ teaspoon salt
- ¼ teaspoon black pepper
- 6 tablespoons oil

Directions:

1. Place the cauliflower florets in a pot with water.
2. Bring to a boil and drain once cooked.
3. Place the cauliflower, eggs, onion, turmeric, salt, and pepper into the food processor.
4. Pulse until the mixture becomes coarse.
5. Transfer into a bowl. Using your hands, form six small flattened balls and place in the fridge for at least 1 hour until the mixture hardens.
6. Heat the oil in a skillet and fry the cauliflower patties for 3 minutes on each side.
7. Serve and enjoy.

Nutrition Info:

- Info Per Servings 2.28g Carbs, 3.9g Protein, 15.3g Fat, 157 Calories

Soups, Stew & Salads Recipes

Brussels Sprouts Salad With Pecorino Romano

Servings: 6
Cooking Time: 35 Minutes
Ingredients:

- 2 lb Brussels sprouts, halved
- 3 tbsp olive oil
- Salt and black pepper to taste
- 2 ½ tbsp balsamic vinegar
- ¼ red cabbage, shredded
- 1 tbsp Dijon mustard
- 1 cup pecorino romano cheese, grated

Directions:

1. Preheat oven to 400ºF and line a baking sheet with foil. Toss the brussels sprouts with olive oil, a little salt, black pepper, and balsamic vinegar, in a bowl, and spread on the baking sheet in an even layer. Bake until tender on the inside and crispy on the outside, about 20 to 25 minutes.
2. Transfer to a salad bowl and add the red cabbage, Dijon mustard and half of the cheese. Mix until well combined. Sprinkle with the remaining cheese, share the salad onto serving plates, and serve with syrup-grilled salmon.

Nutrition Info:

- Info Per Servings 6g Carbs, 4g Protein, 18g Fat, 210 Calories

Corn And Bacon Chowder

Servings: 8
Cooking Time: 23 Minutes
Ingredients:

- ½ cup bacon, fried and crumbled
- 1 package celery, onion, and bell pepper mix
- 2 cups full-fat milk
- ½ cup sharp cheddar cheese, grated
- 5 tablespoons butter
- Pepper and salt to taste
- 1 cup water

Directions:

1. In a heavy-bottomed pot, melt butter.
2. Saute the bacon and celery for 3 minutes.
3. Turn fire on to medium. Add remaining ingredients and cook for 20 minutes until thick.
4. Serve and enjoy with a sprinkle of crumbled bacon.

Nutrition Info:

- Info Per Servings 4.4g Carbs, 16.6g Protein, 13.6g Fat, 210.5 Calories

Simplified French Onion Soup

Servings: 5
Cooking Time: 30 Minutes
Ingredients:

- 3 large onions, sliced
- 2 bay leaves
- 5 cups Beef Bone Broth
- 1 teaspoon dried thyme
- 1-oz Gruyere cheese, sliced into 5 equal pieces
- Pepper to taste
- 4 tablespoons oil

Directions:

1. Place a heavy-bottomed pot on medium-high fire and heat pot for 3 minutes.
2. Add oil and heat for 2 minutes. Stir in onions and sauté for 5 minutes.
3. Lower fire to medium-low, continue sautéing onions for 10 minutes until soft and browned, but not burned.
4. Add remaining ingredients and mix well.
5. Bring to a boil, lower fire to a simmer, cover and cook for 5 minutes.
6. Ladle into bowls, top with cheese.
7. Let it sit for 5 minutes.
8. Serve and enjoy.

Nutrition Info:

- Info Per Servings 9.9g Carbs, 4.3g Protein, 16.8g Fat, 208 Calories

Bacon And Spinach Salad

Servings: 4
Cooking Time: 20 Minutes
Ingredients:

- 2 large avocados, 1 chopped and 1 sliced
- 1 spring onion, sliced
- 4 cooked bacon slices, crumbled
- 2 cups spinach
- 2 small lettuce heads, chopped
- 2 hard-boiled eggs, chopped
- Vinaigrette:
- 3 tbsp olive oil
- 1 tsp Dijon mustard
- 1 tbsp apple cider vinegar

Directions:

1. Combine the spinach, lettuce, eggs, chopped avocado, and spring onion, in a large bowl. Whisk together the vinaigrette ingredients in another bowl.
2. Pour the dressing over, toss to combine and top with the sliced avocado and bacon.

Nutrition Info:

- Info Per Servings 3.4g Carbs, 7g Protein, 33g Fat, 350 Calories

Creamy Cauliflower Soup With Bacon Chips

Servings: 4
Cooking Time: 25 Minutes
Ingredients:
- 2 tbsp ghee
- 1 onion, chopped
- 2 head cauliflower, cut into florets
- 2 cups water
- Salt and black pepper to taste
- 3 cups almond milk
- 1 cup shredded white cheddar cheese
- 3 bacon strips

Directions:
1. Melt the ghee in a saucepan over medium heat and sauté the onion for 3 minutes until fragrant.
2. Include the cauli florets, sauté for 3 minutes to slightly soften, add the water, and season with salt and black pepper. Bring to a boil, and then reduce the heat to low. Cover and cook for 10 minutes.
3. Puree cauliflower with an immersion blender until the ingredients are evenly combined and stir in the almond milk and cheese until the cheese melts. Adjust taste with salt and black pepper.
4. In a non-stick skillet over high heat, fry the bacon, until crispy. Divide soup between serving bowls, top with crispy bacon, and serve hot.

Nutrition Info:
- Info Per Servings 6g Carbs, 8g Protein, 37g Fat, 402 Calories

Arugula Prawn Salad With Mayo Dressing

Servings: 4
Cooking Time: 15 Minutes
Ingredients:
- 4 cups baby arugula
- ½ cup garlic mayonnaise
- 3 tbsp olive oil
- 1 lb tiger prawns, peeled and deveined
- 1 tsp Dijon mustard
- Salt and chili pepper to season
- 2 tbsp lemon juice

Directions:
1. Add the mayonnaise, lemon juice and mustard in a small bowl. Mix until smooth and creamy. Heat 2 tbps of olive oil in a skillet over medium heat, add the prawns, season with salt, and chili pepper, and fry in the oil for 3 minutes on each side until prawns are pink. Set aside to a plate.
2. Place the arugula in a serving bowl and pour half of the dressing on the salad. Toss with 2 spoons until mixed, and add the remaining dressing. Divide salad into 4 plates and serve with prawns.

Nutrition Info:
- Info Per Servings 2g Carbs, 8g Protein, 20.3g Fat, 215 Calories

Traditional Greek Salad

Servings: 4
Cooking Time: 10 Minutes
Ingredients:

- 5 tomatoes, chopped
- 1 large cucumber, chopped
- 1 green bell pepper, chopped
- 1 small red onion, chopped
- 16 kalamata olives, chopped
- 4 tbsp capers
- 1 cup feta cheese, chopped
- 1 tsp oregano, dried
- 4 tbsp olive oil
- Salt to taste

Directions:

1. Place tomatoes, bell pepper, cucumber, onion, feta cheese and olives in a bowl; mix to combine well. Season with salt. Combine capers, olive oil, and oregano, in a small bowl. Drizzle with the dressing to serve.

Nutrition Info:

- Info Per Servings 8g Carbs, 9.3g Protein, 28g Fat, 323 Calories

Lobster Salad With Mayo Dressing

Servings: 4
Cooking Time: 1 Hour 10 Minutes
Ingredients:

- 1 small head cauliflower, cut into florets
- ⅓ cup diced celery
- ½ cup sliced black olives
- 2 cups cooked large shrimp
- 1 tbsp dill, chopped
- Dressing:
- ½ cup mayonnaise
- 1 tsp apple cider vinegar
- ¼ tsp celery seeds
- A pinch of black pepper
- 2 tbsp lemon juice
- 2 tsp swerve
- Salt to taste

Directions:

1. Combine the cauliflower, celery, shrimp, and dill in a large bowl. Whisk together the mayonnaise, vinegar, celery seeds, black pepper, sweetener, and lemon juice in another bowl. Season with salt to taste.
2. Pour the dressing over and gently toss to combine; refrigerate for 1 hour. Top with olives to serve.

Nutrition Info:

- Info Per Servings 2g Carbs, 12g Protein, 15g Fat, 182 Calories

Spinach Fruit Salad With Seeds

Servings: 4

Cooking Time: 1 Hour 10 Minutes

Ingredients:

- 2 tablespoons sesame seeds
- 1 tablespoon poppy seeds
- 1 tablespoon minced onion
- 10 ounces fresh spinach - rinsed, dried and torn into bite-size pieces
- 1 quart strawberries - cleaned, hulled and sliced
- 1/2 cup stevia
- 1/2 cup olive oil
- 1/4 cup distilled white vinegar
- 1/4 teaspoon Worcestershire sauce
- 1/4 teaspoon paprika

Directions:

1. Mix together the spinach and strawberry in a large bowl, stir in the sesame seeds, poppy seeds, stevia, olive oil, vinegar, paprika, Worcestershire sauce and onion in a medium bowl. Cover and cool for 1 hour.

2. Pour dressing over salad to combine well. Serve immediately or refrigerate for 15 minutes.

Nutrition Info:

- Info Per Servings 8.6g Carbs, 6g Protein, 18g Fat, 220 Calories

Sour Cream And Cucumbers

Servings: 8

Cooking Time: 0 Minutes

Ingredients:

- ½ cup sour cream
- 3 tablespoons white vinegar
- 4 medium cucumbers, sliced thinly
- 1 small sweet onion, sliced thinly
- Salt and pepper to taste
- 3 tablespoons olive oil

Directions:

1. In a bowl, whisk the sour cream and vinegar. Season with salt and pepper to taste. Whisk until well-combined.
2. Add in the cucumber and the rest of the ingredients.
3. Toss to coat.
4. Allow chilling before serving.

Nutrition Info:

- Info Per Servings 4.8g Carbs, 0.9g Protein, 8.3g Fat, 96 Calories

Spicy Chicken Bean Soup

Servings: 8

Cooking Time:1h 20 Mins

Ingredients:

- 8 skinless, boneless chicken breast halves
- 5 cubes chicken bouillon
- 2 cans peeled and diced tomatoes
- 1 container sour cream
- 1 cups frozen cut green beans
- 3 tablespoons. olive oil
- Salt and black pepper to taste
- 1 onion, chopped
- 3 cloves garlic, chopped
- 1 cups frozen cut green beans

Directions:

1. Heat olive oil in a large pot over medium heat, add onion, garlic and cook until tender. Stir in water, chicken, salt, pepper, bouillon cubes and bring to boil, simmer for 1 hour on Low. Remove chicken from the pot, reserve 5 cups broth and slice.

2. Stir in the remaining ingredients in the pot and simmer 30 minutes. Serve and enjoy.

Nutrition Info:

- Info Per Servings 7.6g Carbs, 26.5g Protein, 15.3g Fat, 275.1 Calories

Balsamic Cucumber Salad

Servings: 6
Cooking Time: 0 Minutes

Ingredients:

- 1 large English cucumber, halved and sliced
- 1 cup grape tomatoes, halved
- 1 medium red onion, sliced thinly
- ¼ cup balsamic vinaigrette
- ¾ cup feta cheese
- Salt and pepper to taste
- ¼ cup olive oil

Directions:

1. Place all ingredients in a bowl.
2. Toss to coat everything with the dressing.
3. Allow chilling before serving.

Nutrition Info:

- Info Per Servings 9g Carbs, 4.8g Protein, 16.7g Fat, 253 Calories

Beef Reuben Soup

Servings: 6
Cooking Time: 20 Minutes

Ingredients:

- 1 onion, diced
- 6 cups beef stock
- 1 tsp caraway seeds
- 2 celery stalks, diced
- 2 garlic cloves, minced
- 2 cups heavy cream
- 1 cup sauerkraut
- 1 pound corned beef, chopped
- 3 tbsp butter
- 1 ½ cup swiss cheese
- Salt and black pepper, to taste

Directions:

1. Melt the butter in a large pot. Add onion and celery, and fry for 3 minutes until tender. Add garlic and cook for another minute.
2. Pour the beef stock over and stir in sauerkraut, salt, caraway seeds, and add a pinch of pepper. Bring to a boil. Reduce the heat to low, and add the corned beef. Cook for about 15 minutes, adjust the seasoning. Stir in heavy cream and cheese and cook for 1 minute.

Nutrition Info:

- Info Per Servings 8g Carbs, 23g Protein, 37g Fat, 450 Calories

Mexican Soup

Servings: 4
Cooking Time: 25 Minutes

Ingredients:

- 1-pound boneless skinless chicken thighs, cut into 3/4-inch pieces
- 1 tablespoon reduced-sodium taco seasoning
- 1 cup salsa
- 1 carton reduced-sodium chicken broth
- 4 tablespoons olive oil

Directions:

1. In a large saucepan, heat oil over medium-high heat. Add chicken; cook and stir 6-8 minutes or until no longer pink. Stir in taco seasoning.
2. Add remaining ingredients; bring to a boil. Reduce heat; simmer, uncovered, 5 minutes to allow flavors to blend. Skim fat before serving.

Nutrition Info:

- Info Per Servings 5.6g Carbs, 25g Protein, 16.5g Fat, 281 Calories

Green Mackerel Salad

Servings: 2
Cooking Time: 25 Minutes
Ingredients:

- 2 mackerel fillets
- 2 hard-boiled eggs, sliced
- 1 tbsp coconut oil
- 2 cups green beans
- 1 avocado, sliced
- 4 cups mixed salad greens
- 2 tbsp olive oil
- 2 tbsp lemon juice
- 1 tsp Dijon mustard
- Salt and black pepper, to taste

Directions:

1. Fill a saucepan with water and add the green beans and salt. Cook over medium heat for about 3 minutes. Drain and set aside.
2. Melt the coconut oil in a pan over medium heat. Add the mackerel fillets and cook for about 4 minutes per side, or until opaque and crispy. Divide the green beans between two salad bowls. Top with mackerel, egg, and avocado slices.
3. In a bowl, whisk together the lemon juice, olive oil, mustard, salt, and pepper, and drizzle over the salad.

Nutrition Info:

- Info Per Servings 7.6g Carbs, 27.3g Protein, 41.9g Fat, 525 Calories

Power Green Soup

Servings: 6
Cooking Time: 30 Minutes
Ingredients:

- 1 broccoli head, chopped
- 1 cup spinach
- 1 onion, chopped
- 2 garlic cloves, minced
- ½ cup watercress
- 5 cups veggie stock
- 1 cup coconut milk
- 1 tsp salt
- 1 tbsp ghee
- 1 bay leaf
- Salt and black pepper, to taste

Directions:

1. Melt the ghee in a large pot over medium heat. Add onion and cook for 3 minutes. Add garlic and cook for another minute. Add broccoli and cook for an additional 5 minutes.
2. Pour the stock over and add the bay leaf. Close the lid, bring to a boil, and reduce the heat. Simmer for about 3 minutes.
3. In the end, add spinach and watercress, and cook for 3 more minutes. Stir in the coconut cream, salt and pepper. Discard the bay leaf, and blend the soup with a hand blender.

Nutrition Info:

- Info Per Servings 5.8g Carbs, 4.9g Protein, 37.6g Fat, 392 Calories

Cobb Egg Salad In Lettuce Cups

Servings: 4

Cooking Time: 20 Minutes

Ingredients:

- 2 chicken breasts, cut into pieces
- 1 tbsp olive oil
- Salt and black pepper to season
- 6 large eggs
- 1 ½ cups water
- 2 tomatoes, seeded, chopped
- 6 tbsp Greek yogurt
- 1 head green lettuce, firm leaves removed for cups

Directions:

1. Preheat oven to 400ºF. Put the chicken pieces in a bowl, drizzle with olive oil, and sprinkle with salt and black pepper. Mix the ingredients until the chicken is well coated with the seasoning.

2. Put the chicken on a prepared baking sheet and spread out evenly. Slide the baking sheet in the oven and bake the chicken until cooked through and golden brown for 8 minutes, turning once.

3. Bring the eggs to boil in salted water in a pot over medium heat for 6 minutes. Run the eggs in cold water, peel, and chop into small pieces. Transfer to a salad bowl.

4. Remove the chicken from the oven when ready and add to the salad bowl. Include the tomatoes and Greek yogurt; mix evenly with a spoon. Layer two lettuce leaves each as cups and fill with two tablespoons of egg salad each. Serve with chilled blueberry juice.

Nutrition Info:

- Info Per Servings 4g Carbs, 21g Protein, 24.5g Fat, 325 Calories

Sriracha Egg Salad With Mustard Dressing

Servings: 8

Cooking Time: 15 Minutes

Ingredients:

- 10 eggs
- ¾ cup mayonnaise
- 1 tsp sriracha
- 1 tbsp mustard
- ½ cup scallions
- ½ stalk celery, minced
- ½ tsp fresh lemon juice
- ½ tsp sea salt
- ½ tsp black pepper, to taste
- 1 head romaine lettuce, torn into pieces

Directions:

1. Add the eggs in a pan and cover with enough water and boil. Get them from the heat and allow to set for 10 minutes while covered. Chop the eggs and add to a salad bowl.

2. Stir in the remaining ingredients until everything is well combined. Refrigerate until ready to serve.

Nutrition Info:

- Info Per Servings 7.7g Carbs, 7.4g Protein, 13g Fat, 174 Calories

Quail Eggs And Winter Melon Soup

Servings: 6

Cooking Time: 40 Minutes

Ingredients:

- 1-pound pork bones
- 4 cloves of garlic, minced
- 1 onion, chopped
- 1 winter melon, peeled and sliced
- 10 quail eggs, pre-boiled and peeled
- Pepper and salt to taste
- 6 cups water, divided
- Chopped cilantro for garnish (optional)

Directions:

1. Place a heavy-bottomed pot on medium-high fire.
2. Add 5 cups water and pork bones. Season generously with pepper.
3. Bring to a boil, lower fire to a simmer, cover and cook for 30 minutes. Discard bones.
4. Add remaining ingredients except for the cilantro. Cover and simmer for another 10 minutes.
5. Adjust seasoning to taste.
6. Serve and enjoy with cilantro for garnish.

Nutrition Info:

- Info Per Servings 5.6g Carbs, 4.0g Protein, 3.0g Fat, 65 Calories

Shrimp With Avocado & Cauliflower Salad

Servings: 6

Cooking Time: 30 Minutes

Ingredients:

- 1 cauliflower head, florets only
- 1 pound medium shrimp
- ¼ cup + 1 tbsp olive oil
- 1 avocado, chopped
- 3 tbsp chopped dill
- ¼ cup lemon juice
- 2 tbsp lemon zest
- Salt and black pepper to taste

Directions:

1. Heat 1 tbsp olive oil in a skillet and cook the shrimp until opaque, about 8-10 minutes. Place the cauliflower florets in a microwave-safe bowl, and microwave for 5 minutes. Place the shrimp, cauliflower, and avocado in a large bowl.

2. Whisk together the remaining olive oil, lemon zest, juice, dill, and some salt and pepper, in another bowl. Pour the dressing over, toss to combine and serve immediately.

Nutrition Info:

- Info Per Servings 5g Carbs, 15g Protein, 17g Fat, 214 Calories

Celery Salad

Servings: 4

Cooking Time: 0 Minutes

Ingredients:

- 3 cups celery, thinly sliced
- ½ cup parmigiana cheese, shaved
- 1/3 cup toasted walnuts
- 4 tablespoons extra virgin olive oil
- 1 tablespoon red wine vinegar
- Salt and pepper to taste

Directions:

1. Place the celery, cheese, and walnuts in a bowl.
2. In a smaller bowl, combine the olive oil and vinegar. Season with salt and pepper to taste. Whisk to combine everything.
3. Drizzle over the celery, cheese, and walnuts. Toss to coat.

Nutrition Info:

- Info Per Servings 3.6g Carbs, 4.3g Protein, 14g Fat, 156 Calories

Watermelon And Cucumber Salad

Servings: 10
Cooking Time: 0 Minutes

Ingredients:

- ½ large watermelon, diced
- 1 cucumber, peeled and diced
- 1 red onion, chopped
- ¼ cup feta cheese
- ½ cup heavy cream
- Salt to taste
- 5 tbsp MCT or coconut oil

Directions:

1. Place all ingredients in a bowl.
2. Toss everything to coat.
3. Place in the fridge to cool before serving.

Nutrition Info:

- Info Per Servings 2.5g Carbs, 0.9g Protein, 100g Fat, 910 Calories

Creamy Cauliflower Soup With Chorizo Sausage

Servings: 4
Cooking Time: 40 Minutes

Ingredients:

- 1 cauliflower head, chopped
- 1 turnip, chopped
- 3 tbsp butter
- 1 chorizo sausage, sliced
- 2 cups chicken broth
- 1 small onion, chopped
- 2 cups water
- Salt and black pepper, to taste

Directions:

1. Melt 2 tbsp. of the butter in a large pot over medium heat. Stir in onion and cook until soft and golden, about 3-4 minutes. Add cauliflower and turnip, and cook for another 5 minutes.

2. Pour the broth and water over. Bring to a boil, simmer covered, and cook for about 20 minutes until the vegetables are tender. Remove from heat. Melt the remaining butter in a skillet. Add the chorizo sausage and cook for 5 minutes until crispy. Puree the soup with a hand blender until smooth. Taste and adjust the seasonings. Serve the soup in deep bowls topped with the chorizo sausage.

Nutrition Info:

- Info Per Servings 5.7g Carbs, 10g Protein, 19.1g Fat, 251 Calories

Chicken Cabbage Soup

Servings: 6
Cooking Time: 30 Minutes

Ingredients:

- 1 can Italian-style tomatoes
- 3 cups chicken broth
- 1 chicken breast
- ½ head of cabbage, shredded
- 1 packet Italian seasoning mix
- Salt and pepper to taste
- 1 cup water
- 1 tsp oil

Directions:

1. Place a heavy-bottomed pot on medium fire and heat for a minute. Add oil and swirl to coat the bottom and sides of the pot.
2. Pan fry chicken breast for 4 minutes per side. Transfer to a chopping board and cut into ½-inch cubes.
3. Add all ingredients to the pot and stir well.
4. Cover and bring to a boil, lower fire to a simmer, and cook for 20 minutes.
5. Adjust seasoning to taste, serve, and enjoy.

Nutrition Info:

- Info Per Servings 5.6g Carbs, 34.1g Protein, 9.3g Fat, 248 Calories

Creamy Cauliflower Soup

Servings: 4

Cooking Time: 20 Minutes

Ingredients:

- 1 cauliflower head, chopped
- ½ cup onions, chopped
- 4 cups chicken broth
- 1 tablespoon butter
- 1 cup heavy cream
- Pepper and salt to taste

Directions:

1. Place all ingredients in a pot on medium-high fire, except for the heavy cream.
2. Season with salt and pepper to taste.
3. Give a good stir to combine everything.
4. Cover and bring to a boil, and simmer for 15 minutes.
5. With an immersion blender, blend well until smooth and creamy.
6. Stir in heavy cream and continue simmering for another 5 minutes. Adjust seasoning if needed.
7. Serve and enjoy.

Nutrition Info:

- Info Per Servings 7.3g Carbs, 53.9g Protein, 30.8g Fat, 531 Calories

Green Salad With Bacon And Blue Cheese

Servings: 4

Cooking Time: 15 Minutes

Ingredients:

- 2 pack mixed salad greens
- 8 strips bacon
- 1 ½ cups crumbled blue cheese
- 1 tbsp white wine vinegar
- 3 tbsp extra virgin olive oil
- Salt and black pepper to taste

Directions:

1. Pour the salad greens in a salad bowl; set aside. Fry bacon strips in a skillet over medium heat for 6 minutes, until browned and crispy. Chop the bacon and scatter over the salad. Add in half of the cheese, toss and set aside.

2. In a small bowl, whisk the white wine vinegar, olive oil, salt, and black pepper until dressing is well combined. Drizzle half of the dressing over the salad, toss, and top with remaining cheese. Divide salad into four plates and serve with crusted chicken fries along with remaining dressing.

Nutrition Info:

- Info Per Servings 2g Carbs, 4g Protein, 20g Fat, 205 Calories

Desserts And Drinks Recipes

Chocolate Cakes

Servings: 6
Cooking Time: 25 Minutes
Ingredients:
- ½ cup almond flour
- ¼ cup xylitol
- 1 tsp baking powder
- ½ tsp baking soda
- 1 tsp cinnamon, ground
- A pinch of salt
- A pinch of ground cloves
- ½ cup butter, melted
- ½ cup buttermilk
- 1 egg
- 1 tsp pure almond extract
- For the Frosting:
- 1 cup double cream
- 1 cup dark chocolate, flaked

Directions:
1. Preheat the oven to 360°F. Use a cooking spray to grease a donut pan.
2. In a bowl, mix the cloves, almond flour, baking powder, salt, baking soda, xylitol, and cinnamon. In a separate bowl, combine the almond extract, butter, egg, buttermilk, and cream. Mix the wet mixture into the dry mixture. Evenly ladle the batter into the donut pan. Bake for 17 minutes.
3. Set a pan over medium heat and warm double cream; simmer for 2 minutes. Fold in the chocolate flakes; combine until all the chocolate melts; let cool. Spread the top of the cakes with the frosting.

Nutrition Info:
- Info Per Servings 10g Carbs, 4.8g Protein, 20g Fat, 218 Calories

Raspberry Creamy Smoothie

Servings: 1
Cooking Time: 0 Minutes
Ingredients:
- ¼ cup coconut milk
- 1 ½ cups brewed coffee, chilled
- 2 tbsps raspberries
- 2 tbsps avocado meat
- 1 tsp chia seeds
- 2 packets Stevia or more to taste
- 3 tbsps coconut oil

Directions:
1. Add all ingredients in a blender.
2. Blend until smooth and creamy.
3. Serve and enjoy.

Nutrition Info:
- Info Per Servings 8.2g Carbs, 4.9g Protein, 33.2g Fat, 350 Calories

Choco-chia Pudding

Servings: 4

Cooking Time: 5 Minutes

Ingredients:

- ¼ cup fresh or frozen raspberries
- 1 scoop chocolate protein powder
- 1 cup unsweetened almond milk
- 3 tbsp Chia seeds
- 1 tsp Stevia (optional)
- 5 tablespoons coconut oil

Directions:

1. Mix the chocolate protein powder and almond milk.
2. Add the chia seeds and mix well with a whisk or a fork. Add the coconut oil.
3. Flavor with Stevia depending on the desired sweetness.
4. Let it rest for 5 minutes and continue stirring.
5. Serve and enjoy.

Nutrition Info:

- Info Per Servings 10g Carbs, 11.5g Protein, 19.6g Fat, 243.5 Calories

Green Tea Brownies With Macadamia Nuts

Servings: 4

Cooking Time: 28 Minutes

Ingredients:

- 1 tbsp green tea powder
- ¼ cup unsalted butter, melted
- 4 tbsp swerve confectioner's sugar
- A pinch of salt
- ¼ cup coconut flour
- ½ tsp low carb baking powder
- 1 egg
- ¼ cup chopped macadamia nuts

Directions:

1. Preheat the oven to 350ºF and line a square baking dish with parchment paper. Pour the melted butter into a bowl, add sugar and salt, and whisk to combine. Crack the egg into the bowl.
2. Beat the mixture until the egg has incorporated. Pour the coconut flour, green tea, and baking powder into a fine-mesh sieve and sift them into the egg bowl; stir. Add the nuts, stir again, and pour the mixture into the lined baking dish. Bake for 18 minutes, remove and slice into brownie cubes. Serve warm.

Nutrition Info:

- Info Per Servings 2.2g Carbs, 5.2g Protein, 23.1g Fat, 248 Calories

Lemony-avocado Cilantro Shake

Servings: 1

Cooking Time: 0 Minutes

Ingredients:

- ½ cup half and half
- 1 packet Stevia, or more to taste
- ¼ avocado, meat scooped
- 1 tbsp chopped cilantro
- 3 tbsps coconut oil
- 1 ½ cups water

Directions:

1. Add all ingredients in a blender.
2. Blend until smooth and creamy.
3. Serve and enjoy.

Nutrition Info:

- Info Per Servings 8.4g Carbs, 4.4g Protein, 49g Fat, 501 Calories

Smarties Cookies

Servings: 8
Cooking Time: 10 Mins
Ingredients:

- 1/4 cup. butter
- 1/2 cup. almond flour
- 1 tsp. vanilla essence
- 12 oz. bag of smarties
- 1 cup. stevia
- 1/4 tsp. baking powder

Directions:

1. Sift in flour and baking powder in a bowl, then stir through butter and mix until well combined.
2. Whisk in stevia and vanilla essence , stir until thick.
3. Then add the smarties and use your hand to mix and divide into small balls.
4. Bake until completely cooked, about 10 minutes. Let it cool and serve.

Nutrition Info:

- Info Per Servings 20.77g Carbs, 3.7g Protein, 11.89g Fat, 239 Calories

Coconut Macadamia Nut Bombs

Servings: 4
Cooking Time: 0 Mins
Ingredients:

- 2 packets stevia
- 5 tbsps unsweetened coconut powder
- 10 tbsps coconut oil
- 3 tbsps chopped macadamia nuts
- Salt to taste

Directions:

1. Heat the coconut oil in a pan over medium heat. Add coconut powder, stevia and salt, stirring to combined well; then remove from heat.
2. Spoon mixture into a lined mini muffin pan. Place in the freezer for a few hours.
3. Sprinkle nuts over the mixture before serving.

Nutrition Info:

- Info Per Servings 0.2g Carbs, 1.1g Protein, 15.2g Fat, 143 Calories

Hazelnut-lettuce Yogurt Shake

Servings: 1
Cooking Time: 0 Minutes
Ingredients:

- 1 cup whole milk yogurt
- 1 cup lettuce chopped
- 1 tbsp Hazelnut chopped
- 1 packet Stevia, or more to taste
- 1 tbsp olive oil
- 1 cup water

Directions:

1. Add all ingredients in a blender.
2. Blend until smooth and creamy.
3. Serve and enjoy.

Nutrition Info:

- Info Per Servings 8.8g Carbs, 9.4g Protein, 22.2g Fat, 282 Calories

Nutritiously Green Milk Shake

Servings: 1

Cooking Time: 5 Minutes

Ingredients:

- 1 cup coconut cream
- 1 packet Stevia, or more to taste
- 1 tbsp coconut flakes, unsweetened
- 2 cups spring mix salad
- 3 tbsps coconut oil
- 1 cup water

Directions:

1. Add all ingredients in a blender.
2. Blend until smooth and creamy.
3. Serve and enjoy.

Nutrition Info:

- Info Per Servings 10g Carbs, 10.5g Protein, 95.3g Fat, 887 Calories

Raspberry-choco Shake

Servings: 1

Cooking Time: 0 Minutes

Ingredients:

- ¼ cup heavy cream, liquid
- 1 tbsp cocoa powder
- 1 packet Stevia, or more to taste
- ¼ cup raspberries
- 1 ½ cups water

Directions:

1. Add all ingredients in a blender.
2. Blend until smooth and creamy.
3. Serve and enjoy.

Nutrition Info:

- Info Per Servings 11.1g Carbs, 3.8g Protein, 45.0g Fat, 438 Calories

No Nuts Fudge

Servings: 15

Cooking Time: 4 Hours

Ingredients:

- ¼ cup cocoa powder
- ½ teaspoon baking powder
- 1 stick of butter, melted
- 4 tablespoons erythritol
- 6 eggs, beaten
- Salt to taste.

Directions:

1. Mix all ingredients in a slow cooker.
2. Add a pinch of salt.
3. Mix until well combined.
4. Cover pot.
5. Press the low settings and adjust the time to 4 hours.

Nutrition Info:

- Info Per Servings 1.3g Carbs, 4.3g Protein, 12.2g Fat, 132 Calories

Strawberry And Yogurt Smoothie

Servings: 3

Cooking Time: 5 Minutes

Ingredients:

- 1/2 cup yogurt
- 1 cup strawberries
- 1 teaspoon almond milk
- 1 teaspoon lime juice
- 1 1/2 teaspoons stevia

Directions:

1. Place all ingredients in a blender, blender until finely smooth. Serve and enjoy.

Nutrition Info:

- Info Per Servings 6.3g Carbs, 4.6g Protein, 12.4g Fat, 155.2 Calories

Passion Fruit Cheesecake Slices

Servings: 8

Cooking Time: 2 Hours 30 Minutes

Ingredients:

- 1 cup crushed almond biscuits
- ½ cup melted butter
- Filling:
- 1 ½ cups cream cheese
- ¾ cup swerve
- 1 ½ whipping cream
- 1 tsp vanilla bean paste
- 4-6 tbsp cold water
- 1 tbsp gelatin powder
- Passionfruit Jelly
- 1 cup passion fruit pulp
- ¼ cup swerve confectioner's sugar
- 1 tsp gelatin powder
- ¼ cup water, room temperature

Directions:

1. Mix the crushed biscuits and butter in a bowl, spoon into a spring-form pan, and use the back of the spoon to level at the bottom. Set aside in the fridge. Put the cream cheese, swerve, and vanilla paste into a bowl, and use the hand mixer to whisk until smooth; set aside.

2. In a bowl, add 2 tbsp of cold water and sprinkle 1 tbsp of gelatin powder. Let dissolve for 5 minutes. Pour the gelatin liquid along with the whipping cream in the cheese mixture and fold gently.

3. Remove the spring-form pan from the refrigerator and pour over the mixture. Return to the fridge.

4. Repeat the dissolving process for the remaining gelatin and once your out of ingredients, pour the confectioner's sugar, and ¼ cup of water into it. Mix and stir in the passion fruit pulp.

5. Remove the cake again and pour the jelly over it. Swirl the pan to make the jelly level up. Place the pan back into the fridge to cool for 2 hours. When completely set, remove and unlock the spring-pan. Lift the pan from the cake and slice the dessert.

Nutrition Info:

- Info Per Servings 6.1g Carbs, 4.4g Protein, 18g Fat, 287 Calories

Vanilla Chocolate Mousse

Servings: 4
Cooking Time: 30 Minutes
Ingredients:

- 3 eggs
- 1 cup dark chocolate chips
- 1 cup heavy cream
- 1 cup fresh strawberries, sliced
- 1 vanilla extract
- 1 tbsp swerve

Directions:

1. Melt the chocolate in a bowl, in your microwave for a minute on high, and let it cool for 10 minutes.
2. Meanwhile, in a medium-sized mixing bowl, whip the cream until very soft. Add the eggs, vanilla extract, and swerve; whisk to combine. Fold int the cooled chocolate.
3. Divide the mousse between four glasses, top with the strawberry slices and chill in the fridge for at least 30 minutes before serving.

Nutrition Info:

- Info Per Servings 3.7g Carbs, 7.6g Protein, 25g Fat, 370 Calories

Raspberry And Greens Shake

Servings: 1
Cooking Time: 0 Minutes
Ingredients:

- ½ cup half and half
- 1 packet Stevia, or more to taste
- 4 raspberries, fresh
- 1 tbsp macadamia oil
- 1 cup Spinach
- 1 cup water

Directions:

1. Add all ingredients in a blender.
2. Blend until smooth and creamy.
3. Serve and enjoy.

Nutrition Info:

- Info Per Servings 2.7g Carbs, 1.4g Protein, 15.5g Fat, 151 Calories

Brownie Mug Cake

Servings: 1
Cooking Time: 5 Minutes
Ingredients:

- 1 egg, beaten
- ¼ cup almond flour
- ¼ teaspoon baking powder
- 1 ½ tablespoons cacao powder
- 2 tablespoons stevia powder
- A pinch of salt
- 1 teaspoon cinnamon powder
- ¼ teaspoon vanilla extract (optional)

Directions:

1. Combine all ingredients in a bowl until well-combined.
2. Transfer in a heat-proof mug.
3. Place the mug in a microwave.
4. Cook for 2 minutes. Let it sit for another 2 minutes to continue cooking.
5. Serve and enjoy.

Nutrition Info:

- Info Per Servings 4.1g Carbs, 9.1g Protein, 11.8g Fat, 159 Calories

Strawberry Vanilla Shake

Servings: 4
Cooking Time: 2 Minutes
Ingredients:

- 2 cups strawberries, stemmed and halved
- 12 strawberries to garnish
- ½ cup cold unsweetened almond milk
- 2/3 tsp vanilla extract
- ½ cup heavy whipping cream
- 2 tbsp swerve

Directions:

1. Process the strawberries, milk, vanilla extract, whipping cream, and swerve in a large blender for 2 minutes; work in two batches if needed . The shake should be frosty.
2. Pour into glasses, stick in straws, garnish with strawberry halves, and serve.

Nutrition Info:

- Info Per Servings 3.1g Carbs, 16g Protein, 22.6g Fat, 285 Calories

Nutty Arugula Yogurt Smoothie

Servings: 1
Cooking Time: 0 Minutes
Ingredients:

- 1 cup whole milk yogurt
- 1 cup baby arugula
- 3 tbsps avocado oil
- 2 tbsps macadamia nuts
- 1 packet Stevia, or more to taste
- 1 cup water

Directions:

1. Add all ingredients in a blender.
2. Blend until smooth and creamy.
3. Serve and enjoy.

Nutrition Info:

- Info Per Servings 9.4g Carbs, 9.3g Protein, 51.5g Fat, 540 Calories

Blackberry Cheese Vanilla Blocks

Servings: 5
Cooking Time: 20mins
Ingredients:

- ½ cup blackberries
- 6 eggs
- 4 oz mascarpone cheese
- 1 tsp vanilla extract
- 4 tbsp stevia
- 8 oz melted coconut oil
- ½ tsp baking powder

Directions:

1. Except for blackberries, blend all ingredients in a blender until smooth.
2. Combine blackberries with blended mixture and transfer to a baking dish.
3. Bake blackberries mixture in the oven at 320°F for 20 minutes. Serve.

Nutrition Info:

- Info Per Servings 15g Carbs, 13g Protein, 4g Fat, 199 Calories

Walnut Cookies

Servings: 12
Cooking Time: 25 Minutes
Ingredients:

* 1 egg
* 2 cups ground pecans
* ¼ cup sweetener
* ½ tsp baking soda
* 1 tbsp butter
* 20 walnuts halves

Directions:

1. Preheat the oven to 350°F. Mix the ingredients, except the walnuts, until combined. Make 20 balls out of the mixture and press them with your thumb onto a lined cookie sheet. Top each cookie with a walnut half. Bake for about 12 minutes.

Nutrition Info:

* Info Per Servings 0.6g Carbs, 1.6g Protein, 11g Fat, 101 Calories

Coconut-melon Yogurt Shake

Servings: 1
Cooking Time: 0 Minutes
Ingredients:

* ¼ cup half and half
* 3 tbsp coconut oil
* ½ cup melon, slices
* 1 tbsp coconut flakes, unsweetened
* 1 tbsp chia seeds
* 1 ½ cups water
* 1 packet Stevia, or more to taste

Directions:

1. Add all ingredients in a blender.
2. Blend until smooth and creamy.
3. Serve and enjoy.

Nutrition Info:

* Info Per Servings 8g Carbs, 2.4g Protein, 43g Fat, 440 Calories

Brownies With Coco Milk

Servings: 10
Cooking Time: 6 Hours
Ingredients:

* ¾ cup coconut milk
* 1 teaspoon erythritol
* 2 tablespoons butter, melted
* 4 egg yolks, beaten
* 5 tablespoons cacao powder

Directions:

1. In a bowl, mix well all ingredients.
2. Lightly grease your slow cooker with cooking spray and pour in batter.
3. Cover and cook on low for six hours.
4. Serve and enjoy.

Nutrition Info:

* Info Per Servings 1.2g Carbs, 1.5g Protein, 8.4g Fat, 86 Calories

Green And Fruity Smoothie

Servings: 2
Cooking Time: 0 Minutes
Ingredients:

- 1 cup spinach, packed
- ½ cup strawberries, chopped
- ½ avocado, peeled, pitted, and frozen
- 1 tbsp almond butter
- ¼ cup packed kale, stem discarded, and leaves chopped
- 1 cup ice-cold water
- 5 tablespoons MCT oil or coconut oil

Directions:

1. Blend all ingredients in a blender until smooth and creamy.
2. Serve and enjoy.

Nutrition Info:

- Info Per Servings 10g Carbs, 1.6g Protein, 47.3g Fat, 459 Calories

Granny Smith Apple Tart

Servings: 8
Cooking Time: 65 Minutes
Ingredients:

- 6 tbsp butter
- 2 cups almond flour
- 1 tsp cinnamon
- ⅓ cup sweetener
- Filling:
- 2 cups sliced Granny Smith
- ¼ cup butter
- ¼ cup sweetener
- ½ tsp cinnamon
- ½ tsp lemon juice
- Topping:
- ¼ tsp cinnamon
- 2 tbsp sweetener

Directions:

1. Preheat your oven to 370ºF and combine all crust ingredients in a bowl. Press this mixture into the bottom of a greased pan. Bake for 5 minutes.
2. Meanwhile, combine the apples and lemon juice in a bowl and let them sit until the crust is ready. Arrange them on top of the crust. Combine the rest of the filling ingredients, and brush this mixture over the apples. Bake for about 30 minutes.
3. Press the apples down with a spatula, return to oven, and bake for 20 more minutes. Combine the cinnamon and sweetener, in a bowl, and sprinkle over the tart.
4. Note: Granny Smith apples have just 9.5g of net carbs per 100g. Still high for you? Substitute with Chayote squash, which has the same texture and rich nutrients, and just around 4g of net carbs .

Nutrition Info:

- Info Per Servings 6.7g Carbs, 7g Protein, 26g Fat, 302 Calories

No Bake Lemon Cheese-stard

Servings: 8
Cooking Time: 0 Minutes
Ingredients:

- 1 tsp vanilla flavoring
- 1 tbsp lemon juice
- 2 oz heavy cream
- 8 oz softened cream cheese
- 1 tsp liquid low carb sweetener (Splenda)
- 1 tsp stevia

Directions:

1. Mix all ingredients in a large mixing bowl until the mixture has a pudding consistency.
2. Pour the mixture to small serving cups and refrigerate for a few hours until it sets.
3. Serve chilled.

Nutrition Info:

- Info Per Servings 1.4g Carbs, 2.2g Protein, 10.7g Fat, 111 Calories

Creamy Choco Shake

Servings: 1
Cooking Time: 0 Minutes
Ingredients:

- ½ cup heavy cream
- 2 tbsp cocoa powder
- 1 packet Stevia, or more to taste
- 1 cup water
- 3 tbsps coconut oil

Directions:

1. Add all ingredients in a blender.
2. Blend until smooth and creamy.
3. Serve and enjoy.

Nutrition Info:

- Info Per Servings 7.9g Carbs, 3.2g Protein, 64.6g Fat, 582 Calories

Appendix : Recipes Index

A

B

Bell Pepper

Corn And Bacon Chowder 62

Blackberry

Blackberry Cheese Vanilla Blocks 79

Broccoli

Colorful Vegan Soup 56

Vegetable Tempura 59

Power Green Soup 68

Brussels Sprout

Sautéed Brussels Sprouts 10

Mixed Roast Vegetables 13

Roasted Brussels Sprouts With Sunflower Seeds 53

Brussels Sprouts Salad With Pecorino Romano 62

C

Carrot

Parsnip And Carrot Fries With Aioli 7

Cauliflower

Bacon Mashed Cauliflower 7

Simple Tender Crisp Cauli-bites 14

Shrimp And Cauliflower Jambalaya 45

Grilled Cauliflower 50

Cauliflower Mac And Cheese 50

Keto Cauliflower Hash Browns 53

Grated Cauliflower With Seasoned Mayo 54

Greek Styled Veggie-rice 61

Cauliflower Fritters 61

Creamy Cauliflower Soup With Bacon Chips 71

Lobster Salad With Mayo Dressing 65

Creamy Cauliflower Soup With Chorizo Sausage 71

Creamy Cauliflower Soup 64

Cheese

Spiced Gruyere Crisps 6

Simplified French Onion Soup 63

Traditional Greek Salad 65

Celery Salad 70

No Bake Lemon Cheese-stard 82

Cherry Tomato

Sausage Links With Tomatoes & Pesto 21

Chicken

Avocado Cheese Pepper Chicken 30

Chicken Chipotle 31

Roast Chicken With Herb Stuffing 36

Chicken Breast

Pacific Chicken 28

Spinach Artichoke Heart Chicken 29

Cheesy Chicken Bake With Zucchini 32

Cilantro Chicken Breasts With Mayo-avocado Sauce 33

Chicken Country Style 33

One Pot Chicken Alfredo 34

Chicken Garam Masala 35

Chicken Breasts With Cheddar & Pepperoni 35

Yummy Chicken Queso 36

Chicken Curry 37

Cheese Stuffed Chicken Breasts With Spinach 37

Red Wine Chicken 38

Baked Pecorino Toscano Chicken 38

Spicy Chicken Bean Soup 66

Cobb Egg Salad In Lettuce Cups 69

Chicken Cabbage Soup 71

Chicken Drumstick

Chicken Paella With Chorizo 32

Chicken Tender

Easy Bbq Chicken And Cheese 29

Chicken Thighs

Easy Chicken Vindaloo 28

Paprika Chicken With Cream Sauce 30

Zesty Grilled Chicken 31

Oven-baked Skillet Lemon Chicken 38

Mexican Soup 67

Chicken Wing

Old Bay Chicken Wings 14

D

Bacon Jalapeno Poppers 11

K

Kale

Creamy Kale And Mushrooms 55

L

Lemon

Flounder With Dill And Capers 41

Lettuce

Middle Eastern Style Tuna Salad 8

Bacon And Spinach Salad 63

Sriracha Egg Salad With Mustard Dressing 69

Hazelnut-lettuce Yogurt Shake 75

M

Macadamia Nut

Green Tea Brownies With Macadamia Nuts 74

Coconut Macadamia Nut Bombs 75

Mackerel

Green Mackerel Salad 68

Mussel

Coconut Curry Mussels 39

P

Pork

Pork Osso Bucco 19

Easy Thai 5-spice Pork Stew 25

Quail Eggs And Winter Melon Soup 70

Pork Chop

Paprika Pork Chops 17

Creamy Pork Chops 17

Garlic Pork Chops With Mint Pesto 20

Pork Loin

Spiced Pork Roast With Collard Greens 16

Pork Loin Chop

Balsamic Grilled Pork Chops 24

Shrimp With Avocado & Cauliflower Salad 70

Skirt Steak

Adobo Beef Fajitas 26

Sour Cream

Sour Cream And Carrot Sticks 15

Spaghetti Squash

Spaghetti Squash With Eggplant & Parmesan 51

Spanish Chorizo

Crispy Chorizo With Cheesy Topping 6

Spinach

Creamy Artichoke And Spinach 55

Spinach Fruit Salad With Seeds 66

Green And Fruity Smoothie 81

Strawberry

Strawberry And Yogurt Smoothie 77

Strawberry Vanilla Shake 79

T

Tilapia Fillet

Buttery Almond Lemon Tilapia 39

Tilapia With Olives & Tomato Sauce 40

Turkey

Turkey & Leek Soup 31

Turkey Breast

Tender Turkey Breast 34

Turnip

Creamy Almond And Turnip Soup 51

W

Walnut

Walnut Cookies 80

Choco And Coconut Bars 10

Coconut And Chocolate Bars 13

Y

Yogurt

Z

Zucchini

Made in the USA
Coppell, TX
07 November 2023

23938410R00057